THE HANDBOOK OF POLICY CREATIVITY, VOLUME I

CREATIVITY AT THE CUTTING EDGE

THE HANDBOOK OF POLICY CREATIVITY, VOLUME I

CREATIVITY AT THE CUTTING EDGE

STUART NAGEL (EDITOR)

Nova Science Publishers, Inc.
Huntington, NY

Senior Editors: Susan Boriotti and Donna Dennis
Coordinating Editor: Tatiana Shohov
Office Manager: Annette Hellinger
Graphics: Wanda Serrano
Book Production: Matthew Kozlowski, Jonathan Rose and Jennifer Vogt
Circulation: Cathy DeGregory, Ave Maria Gonzalez, Ron Hedges
and Andre Tillman

Library of Congress Cataloging-in-Publication Data
Available Upon Request

ISBN 1-59033-030-7.

Copyright © 2001 by Nova Science Publishers, Inc.
227 Main Street, Suite 100
Huntington, New York 11743
Tele. 631-424-6682   Fax 631-425-5933
E Mail: Novascience@earthlink.net

Dedicated to people I have worked with in recent years
who have stimulated my creativity
by doing collaborative drafting such as
(1) Carol Burger, (2) Deni Hoffman,
(3) Yuki Llewellyn, and (4) Dixie Trinkle
and by doing desktop publishing such as
(1) Diem-My Bui, (2) Sara Eckart,
(3) Sharon Jiwon Kim Hudson, and (4) Amy Robb.

CONTENTS

LIST OF TABLES AND FIGURES

PART ONE: BASIC CONCEPTS

Chapter 1

CREATIVITY AND RELATED CONCEPTS

Stuart Nagel

The concept of creativity (as used in the *C+ News*) sometimes gets confused with other related concepts. We define creativity as being usefully innovative in solving diverse problems.

This creativity concept should be distinguished from the following eight concepts:

1. THINKING. This is a process whereby one mentally manipulates images or words. The manipulation is not necessarily innovative and not necessarily useful. Creativity generally involves thinking, but it may be a reflex reaction with only a split second between confronting a problem and coming up with an innovative, useful solution.

2. REASONING. This is a process whereby one goes from a problem to a solution by generalizing from previous instances (inductive reasoning), or by deducing from analogous examples or relevant principles (deductive reasoning). Reasoning may also not necessarily involve anything innovative or especially useful. An example is reasoning that, if one has four apples and one is taken away, then one will have three apples. Creativity generally involves reasoning, but not necessarily, since much creativity seems to be intuitive or even emotional. Creativity is like generating explanatory hypotheses. It does not tell us how to generate hypotheses. Testing them may involve rational reasoning in accordance with the principles for testing causation devised by John Stuart Mill. Generating hypotheses is not so likely to involve rational reasoning, as contrasted to having a flash of insight. Such flashes, however, can be facilitated by such things as knowing the subject matter, being wide awake, and having big stakes involved, meaning rewards for success and punishments for failure.

3. PRODUCTIVITY. This is a process whereby one gets a lot of units of work done in a short time or with little money. One can be highly productive and neither

innovative or useful, as when one produces lots of junk mail, pulls on a slot machine, or games of tic-tac-toe or chess. Productivity is relevant to creativity because being creative does not mean much if one does not implement one's creativity. Implementing is another word for producing results or being productive.

4. INNOVATION. This involves something new, but not necessarily useful. A person is not generally referred to as being creative (as Edison was) if all they innovate are neologisms or new wordy jargon. Likewise, working out the implications of a new form of checkers that involves 128 squares instead of 64 squares does not sound very useful, although it would be a new form of checkers.

5. USEFULNESS. This is part of our definition of creativity. The word useful only needs to be defined in the context in which we use it, which refers to the clause "being usefully innovative in solving diverse problems."

6. PROBLEMS. Any situation that has alternatives or choices that need to be chosen is a problem. Some problems, however, are more important than other problems. Thus the problems of what to do about global violence, poverty, dictatorship, disease, and illiteracy are more important than the problem of how the Chicago Cubs can win the pennant, although the Chicago Cubs are also a problem.

7. CHOOSING. Since creativity involves solving problems, it therefore involves choosing, but not all choosing is creative. When one chooses bacon and eggs rather than ham and eggs for breakfast, that is not being creative. Once again, we are back to our original definition of creativity which requires being usefully innovative in solving diverse problems. Choosing from a breakfast menu may be useful but probably not likely to be very innovative.

8. DEGREES. Notice the word "very" before "innovative" because innovativeness has degrees just as usefulness does. In fact, all the sub-concepts of creativity have degrees. There are degrees of "solving", degrees of "diversity", and degrees of importance and difficulty in "problems" as well as degrees of usefulness and innovativeness.

One useful purpose served by editing or contributing to *Creativity Plus* is that it helps to clarify one's ideas about creativity. In fact, one can say that one of the best ways to creatively solve diverse problems is to try to explain to others how to solve diverse problems. *Creativity Plus* will try to give lots of opportunities to potential contributors to do exactly that.

Chapter 2

CREATIVE PEOPLE

Harriet Zuckerman
Andrew Mellon Foundation

I. SELECTION

That the Nobel prize now serves as the prime symbol of achievement in science and outside is consistent with Alfred Nobel's intent, although he could scarcely have foreseen how far social process would outrun that intent. He wanted to promote human welfare, to honor great accomplishment, and, above all, to foster research by providing "such complete economic independence for those who by their previous work had given promise to further achievement that they could ever afterwards devote themselves entirely to research."

These announced purposes were in large part a function of the particular time and place in the development of science. In the late nineteenth century, there was no substantial support for research, and comparatively few scientists were employed as researchers. As an inventor and scientist of sorts, Nobel knew from his own experience that costs of most research were modest. It was not unrealistic for him to believe that he could accomplish the double purpose of underwriting the work of a handful of first-class scientists and providing for their support as well. As late as 1920, for example, the research grant for the entire Cavendish Laboratory was only 2,000 pounds, or about ten thousand dollars. But when the Nobel prizes were inaugurated in 1901, the awards came to $42,000 each. By way of comparison, this was seventy times as large as the honorarium attached to the Royal Society's Rumford Medal, one of the major prizes in science available at the time. For the general public, the Nobel's princely sum constituted a symbolic message asserting in a way that could be understood by the informed and uninformed alike that science and scientists really mattered. For many of the scientists themselves, it provided both symbolic and public recognition within their own ranks of major contributions to scientific knowledge.

When Nobel set down the requirements for his prizes in science, he stipulated that they be given in just three fields: physics, chemistry, and physiology or medicine. Mathematicians like to explain the absence of a Nobel prize in mathematics by telling the story of the rivalry between Alfred Nobel and the Swedish mathematician, Gosta Mittag-Leffler, for the hand of an unidentified lady. Nobel, the story goes, was the unsuccessful suitor. By excluding mathematics from the fields eligible for prizes, Nobel retaliated and made sure that Mittag-Leffler would never get one of his prizes. Appealing as the story is, it seems to be more fantasy than fact. It appears in none of the standard histories of mathematics nor can a number of historically minded mathematicians say just where they encountered it or even that it is consistent with what they know of Mittag-Leffler's private life. One might better conclude, along with Stig Ramel of the Nobel Foundation, that Nobel excluded mathematics from the fields to be covered by the prizes because he wanted to benefit mankind in a concrete, rather than abstract, way.

Each prize was to be given for "discoveries," "inventions," or "improvements" (the language varies for each science) made "during the preceding year," and nationality was not to be taken into account in the process of selection.) He left it up to his executors, the Royal Swedish Academy of Sciences and the Royal Caroline Institute, to draw up the detailed rules that would govern the actual selection of recipients. It took five years for the interested parties (including the Nobel relatives) to agree on procedures and the wording of the official statutes and to make the first selections. Since then, elaborate customs have evolved about the selection of candidates and the conferring of the awards by the king of Sweden in Stockholm, but the statutes themselves have not changed.

Although the statutes governing selection of prize-winners differ somewhat for the awards given by the Academy and by the Caroline Institute, in their essentials they are the same. Most important, the statutes provide for the establishment of three committees, each comprised of five qualified scientists who have primary responsibility for inviting nominations, investigating candidates, and selecting the winners. The names of those selected are presented for formal approval to the membership of the Academy and the faculty of the Caroline Institute on specified dates. Committee members serve for renewable terms of three to five years and are elected by the Academy for physics and chemistry and by the Institute for medicine and physiology. The physics and chemistry committees always include the chiefs of the physics and chemistry sections of the Nobel Institute, and the committee for physiology and medicine includes the rector of the Caroline Institute. Since the committees determine who can nominate in a given year and since they control the evaluation process, their power to select and reject potential laureates should be evident.

Nominations are solicited from two sets of proposers: those with permanent rights to nominate (members of the Academy of Sciences, the faculties of the Caroline Institute and of the eight Scandinavian universities in the appropriate sciences, and past laureates) and others who are invited to do so year by year. In 1900, when the first nominations were solicited, the committees supervising the prizes in physics and chemistry each sent out 300 invitations. Now, upward of a thousand scientists the world over are asked to nominate for each of the prizes although far fewer actually do so. The committees hold that they systematically solicit nominations from scientists at minor as well as major research centers.

Nominators may propose several candidates, but the prizes may not be divided into more than three shares, presumably so as to maintain the honor and the honorarium at the level Nobel intended. Thus far, this has meant that laureates are laureates whether or not they have shared their prizes. In effect, no laureate is a fractional Nobel prize-winner. Beyond this, all nominees must be alive not only at the time they are proposed but also at the time the award is made. Prizes in the sciences are never given posthumously.

The application of these rather simple procedures for nomination and selection has produced a distinguished roster of Nobel laureates in science. As we shall see, however, these same procedures leave room for complaint and skepticism about the preeminent award in science.

II. INDICATORS OF EXCELLENCE

The significance of the laureates' scientific contributions and of their standing in the scientific community can be roughly gauged by four indicators: the impact of their research before receiving the prize; their overall versatility as investigators, some having made not one but several contributions considered to be prizeworthy; the extent of consensus among nominators for the prizes; and the continuing influence of the laureate's work after it was honored by the prize.

A. Impact of Research by Future Laureates

In the aggregate future Nobel laureates have greatly influenced ongoing research in their fields as can be seen in part from an analysis of citations to their published work. With all their limitations, citation counts have been found to be a useful though crude indicator of the impact of research on subsequent scientific development. In terms of this measure, laureates-to-be, scientists who we know by hindsight will win Nobel prizes, have been among the most influential of contemporary scientists. Their work is heavily cited – in fact, almost forty times as often as the average author whose research has been cited at all and who therefore is listed in the Science Citation Index. Laureates named between 1965 and 1969, for example, averaged 232 citations in the 1965 index as compared with an average of six citations to other scientific authors listed there. This rate of citation placed 85 percent of the laureates-to-be among the top 0.2 percent of authors cited in the scientific literature that year. Not surprisingly, laureates-to-be also frequently turn up on the Science Citation Index list of the fifty most cited authors. Four on the 1967 list – Gell-Mann, Herzberg, von Euler, and Barton – were to win Nobel prizes in the next five years.

As measured by citations, the impact of research by future laureates plainly derives from their considerable overall scientific productivity, but they also rank high among authors of the individual papers most frequently cited in the science literature. Of the fifty papers most often cited in 1967 – the first year for which such data are available – five are by laureates-to-be: Gell-Mann, Bardeen, Cooper, Schrieffer, Moore, and Stein. Since papers reporting new methods or research instruments tend to be cited more often than theoretical or experimental contributions, the fact that future laureates' papers appear on this list at all testifies to the substantial impact of their research. Some papers by prospective laureates also become "landmarks" in the sense of being much used and long lived. They are frequently cited for years and do not exhibit the usual pattern of declining citation soon after publication. The paper Nirenberg and Matthaei published on the genetic code in 1961, for example, was cited more than a hundred times between 1964 and 1968, when Nirenberg got his prize. Gell-Mann's paper on symmetries of baryons and mesons, published in 1962, was cited about 150 times a year in the same period. All this suggests that the scientific work of laureates has been enormously influential before they received their prizes. So much for these quantitatively crude estimates of the impact of research by future laureates.

B. Multiple Prize-Worthy Contributions

Although some laureates have focused on a single line of investigation, most have moved from problem to problem, making diverse contributions sometimes to quite distinct fields of inquiry. When scientists do several pieces of fundamental work, their candidacy for a Nobel prize is validated. The fact that the same investigator has done several important things reduces disagreement about selecting him if not about the merits of the particular contribution for which he received an award. There is, for instance, the case of Otto Warburg, whose research on the Pasteur reaction survived the rigorous selection process and was judged by the committee for the prize in medicine to be "prize-worthy" in 1927. Such judgments are kept confidential since, by statute, the committees deliberate in secret. But the rule of silence was once breached by Göran Liljestrand, official historian of the prize in medicine, in his published review of awards in that field. It was there that he named sixty-nine scientists, among them Warburg, whose work had been officially, if secretly, judged to be prize-worthy. Ironically, Warburg lost out that year to Johannes Fibiger, one of the most conspicuous Nobel "errors." But, by 1931, Warburg had produced another contribution on the respiratory enzyme that was also judged to be prize-worthy and for which he won his award. In 1944, he was nominated for a Nobel prize once again, this time for his studies of the role of enzymes in intermediary metabolism, but the Committee decided not to make a second award. Warburg, then, could have been named a laureate on any (or all) of three occasions, and this multiplication of eligible contributions confirmed his standing as a laureate.

The most consequential scientists are of course those who have made several fundamental contributions. To take an obvious instance, Einstein won an award in 1921 for his discovery of the photoelectric effect. His monumental work in 1905 on the special theory of relativity and the theory of Brownian motion and in 1916 on the general theory of relativity were not mentioned in the prize citation, but they would have surely gained a prize for him later had his work on the photoelectric effect been considered ineligible. Or take the case of Edward C. Kendall whose research on thyroxin (between 1914 and 1926) was proposed for the prize in medicine and judged prize-worthy. Kendall, however, did not win his prize for the thyroxin investigations; they were, for unknown reasons, passed by. He had to wait until 1950 to become a laureate, when his studies of the biochemistry of cortisone and its use in treating chronic rheumatoid arthritis finally brought him a publicly visible award. The list of multiple near laureates, scientists who qualified several times for the Nobel prize, also includes the biologists Robert Koch and Paul Ehrlich, the biochemists Emil Fischer and Adolph Windaus, and the chemist J. H. van't Hoff. But the career of Frederick Soddy provides the clearest case of one laureate's multiple prize-worthy contributions.

As a close, indispensable collaborator of William Ramsay, Soddy nonetheless did not share in the chemistry prize that Ramsay won in 1904. Soddy missed out again four years later when the prize went to Ernest Rutherford, even though Rutherford emphatically stated that Soddy had been a full collaborator on the research cited for his award. Soddy finally received his own prize in 1921 for his investigations of isotopes, thus demonstrating his persistence and putting to rest questions that had been raised about the wisdom of the Chemistry Committee's earlier decisions. The ultimate cases of validation of Nobel selections are of course Marie Curie and John Bardeen, the only researchers to have won two Nobel prizes in science.

C. Consensus on Nominations

As gauged by the clustering of nominations, there has been marked consensus on the merits of many scientists nominated for a prize. This includes multiple nominations in the same year for one or more candidates as well as their repeated nomination year after year. Although there is evidence that campaigns have been mounted for one or another candidate (a matter to be discussed later), there is no reason to suppose that nominators did not believe in the merits of the candidates for whom campaigns had been waged. Arne Tiselius, once chairman of the Chemistry Committee, president of the Foundation, and laureate in chemistry, has remarked from his distinctive vantage point that "despite [the] system of circulation of invitations for nomination of candidates, certain names appear year after year, not so few of them. ...As a whole our experience would indicate that there is an international opinion about who represents the elite in certain fields."

Since the Nobel committees remain silent about the names proposed for awards, systematic data on the extent of agreement among nominators are unavailable. But the public record does occasionally contain gross statistics on nominations for particular years and, now and then, the names of scientists nominated many times. From these scattered clues, we can piece together some information on the extent of agreement on nominations.

In the first years of the prizes, there was considerable agreement. Roentgen, the first laureate in physics, received seventeen out of twenty-nine nominations and van't Hoff, the first winner in chemistry, eleven out of twenty. In 1904, Ramsay won twenty-two out of thirty-two nominations, and in the following two years Adolph von Baeyer and Henri

Moissan also received a majority of nominations for the prize in chemistry. Once the backlog of distinguished scientists was exhausted the extent of agreement declined although a measure of consensus about certain candidates recurs. Thus, to take an extreme case, the neurophysiologist C. S. Sherrington received a cumulative total of 134 nominations from thirteen countries over a span of thirty years, until he finally got the prize in medicine in 1932. The question remains, of course, why the Committee waited so long to recognize Sherrington's work.

Evidently scientists who have been passed over in a given year are not "lost causes." In the case of the prize in medicine, at least two thirds of the nominees each year have been proposed before. This is less often the case in chemistry, where about a third of the candidates are renominations. Gauged by the frequency of multiple nominations and of renominations, consensus apparently obtains for a significant fraction of candidates. Although it appears that many scientists chosen for a prize have been candidates for some time, the committees insist that they are not influenced by the number of times a candidate has been nominated.

D. Enduring Influence of Laureates' Research

Finally, the quality of laureates' contributions can be assessed in terms of their continuing scientific impact. Such "after-the-fact" validation of decisions by the Nobel committees does not result merely from the halo effect of the prize, as we shall see. Most laureates who received prizes between 1901 and 1964 still appear often in the Science Citation Index. Their mean of ninety-seven citations each in 1965 places them within the top 1 percent of all scientists cited in the index (but significantly below the laureates-to-be who were selected later on and were cited an average of 232 times that year, as indicated earlier). Although the work of prospective laureates should break new ground, according to the conventional wisdom about the mortality of research, the work of past laureates should be thoroughly outdated. But on the whole they are not conventional scientists, and conventional wisdom fails to meet their case. At least some of their research continues to be used. Among the fifty most cited authors listed in the Science Citation Index from its inception in 1961 to 1972 are 13 Nobel prize-winners, including some "old timers" such as Max Born, whose important work on the statistical interpretation of the wave function dates back to 1926.

Another indication of the significance of laureates' research is the frequency with which they are singled out by fellow scientists as having made important contributions. Stephen Cole found for a sample of some 300 American biochemists, physicists, and chemists that laureates rank consistently high in lists of the "five scientists who have contributed most to the field in the last fifteen years." Although the laureates comprised only 23 percent of the names given in response to Cole's question, they received 63 percent of the mentions. That is, each of the laureates listed received an average of 10.8 mentions as compared with 1.9 each for all other scientists. The top-ranking scientist in each of the three fields is a laureate, as were all ten of the top-ranking biochemists, nine of the ten top-ranking physicists (Brian Josephson, the tenth, having since won his prize), and, for possibly interesting though unknown reasons, "only" half of the ten ranking chemists.

Like the other indicators, Cole's data testify that the contributions of laureates have continuing relevance for the development of scientific knowledge. This has further ramified consequences. For one thing, the merit of their scientific work and the consequent esteem accorded them contribute to the prestige of the Nobel prize that, in turn, confers enhanced prestige upon the later recipients. For another, the Nobel prize itself has come to symbolize great scientific achievement for scientists as well as laymen. Often enough, scientists can be overheard remarking that a colleague "should have the prize" or "will surely win the prize." Such remarks are easily misunderstood by outsiders, who conclude that the prize itself has paramount importance. In fact, these remarks indicate that the prize is used as a shorthand for a certain level of accomplishment. At the same time, there is evidence that scientists are increasingly skeptical about the Nobel, in no small measure because they know that excellent work is not confined to the ranks of the laureates.

NOTES

1. From Harriet Zuckerman, *Scientific Elite: Nobel Laureates in the United States* (Transaction Publishers, 1996 and Free Press, 1977). The book contains many supportive references. Harriet Zuckerman is a Professor Emeritus of Sociology at Columbia University

Chapter 3

CREATIVE PEOPLE IN THE
SECOND AND THIRD MILLENNIA

Stuart Nagel

Creativity Plus likes to talk about causes and effects of creativity. It also likes to talk about examples of creativity and creative people. Two recent publications attempt to list the 100 most creative people for the second millennium of 1000-2000 and the third millennium of 2000-3000.

I. THE SECOND MILLENNIUM 1000-2000

The first publication covers the second millennium. It is entitled *Biography of the Millennium: 100 People, 1000 Years*. It is from a survey of experts by the A&E Television Networks. It may overemphasize the last 100 years and creative Americans, but it still seems quite appropriate and interesting. The tapes can be obtained from the A&E World, 19 Gregory Drive, South Burlington, VT 05403.

The creative people are not grouped, but one can group them into such categories as (1) scientists and inventors from natural and social science, (2) artists from music, literature, and visual arts, (3) political and military figures from all over the world, and (4) miscellaneous creative people.

What they all have in common is being highly creative in their respective fields with substantial impact on subsequent human activity. Some of these creative people were evil such as Hitler and Stalin. They may, however, not meet the definition of creativity since creativity is defined as being usefully innovative, and evil is the opposite of useful. The A&E people do not refer to the list of 100 people as being creative. The people are referred to as being "greatest," most admired," unforgettable personalities," "profoundly significant," and "changed our world in ways beyond imagining," all in one descriptive paragraph.

The top 20 people in rank order are:

1. Johann Gutenberg c1400-1468. Inventor of printing press.
2. Isaac Newton 1642-1727. Master of mathematics, physics, scientific revolution.
3. Martin Luther 1383-1546. Leader Protestant Revolution. Faith for salvation.
4. Charles Darwin 1809-1882. Theory of Evolution
5. William Shakespeare 1564-1616. World's most famous writer.
6. Christopher Columbus 1451-1506. Spread culture of Europe to America.
7. Karl Marx 1818-1883. Evil capitalism. Working class would rise from oppression.
8. Albert Einstein 1879-1955. Theory of Relativity, Worked for peace.
9. Nicolaus Copernicus 1479-1543. Understanding of solar system.
10. Galileo 1564-1642. Science of modern astronomy.
11. Leonardo Da Vinci 1452-1519. Renaissance man.
12. Sigmund Freud 1856-1939. Exploration of the mind and psychotherapy.
13. Louis Pasteur 1822-1895. Pasteurization and vaccine for rabies.
14. Thomas Edison 1847-1931. Great inventor, e.g., electric light, motion pictures.
15. Thomas Jefferson 1743-1826. Declaration of Independence and Bill of Rights.
16. Adolph Hitler 1889-1945. Overthrow of Europe, Nazism, Holocaust.
17. Mahatma Gandhi 1869-1948. Non-violent civil disobedience.
18. John Locke 1632-1704. Life, liberty, property, and pursuit of happiness.
19. Michelangelo 1475-1564. Renaissance art, e.g., St. Peter's Cathedral.
20. Adam Smith 1723-1790. Economic theory of free trade and capitalism.

II. THE THIRD MILLENNIUM 2000-3000

The second publication covers the third millennium. It is entitled *A View from the Year 3000: A Ranking of the 100 Most Influential Persons at the End of the Year 2999*. It is authored by Arturo Kukeni which is the pseudonym for Michael Hart. The book is published by Poseidon Press. This list especially emphasizes people who invent solutions to 1999 problems, but who do so over the next thousand years.

Just as the A&E book emphasizes the 1900's, this book probably emphasizes the first 100 years of the third millennium. That is not because 2000-2100 is the most creative century of the third millennium. On the contrary, subsequent centuries are likely to be more creative in view of how new inventions are occurring at an exponential rate or a geometric progression. Each new invention tends to roughly generate two others. There may be a plateauing out for narrowly defined fields like the automobile, the airplane, the radio, and the television set, but there is new growth in their broader fields of transportation and communication. Technological and other change is also explosive if one combines the S-shaped curves for all the narrowly defined fields before they plateau out.

The reason for the emphasis on the first century of the third millennium is because the likely happenings after 2100 are probably beyond our present comprehension. People in the year 1000 probably could not comprehend what has happened in the 1900's or any 100 years subsequent to the Renaissance or the Industrial Revolution.

To make the futurist list shorter and more useful, we have eliminated the names of people, their birthdates, and when they died. Instead, each person is designated as X1, X2, X3, and so on. Ten of the 100 creative people from 2000-3000 are listed below. They were chosen by Michael Marien, the editor of the *Future Survey* in reviewing the Kukeni book in the October issue of the *Future Survey*.

X1   The most influential person in history who brought us immortality by growing new brain tissue in vitro and uploading all memory and personality into computers.

X2   Who devised a method of downloading information into the human brain so as to achieve desired personality changes.

X3   Who led a rebellion against a would-be global dictator.

X4   Who devised a set of safe, quick, and completely reversible techniques for sex-change.

X11 Primarily responsible for designing the constitutional system of the world government.

X22 Inventor of the first practical system for generating cheap power by nuclear fusion.

X23 The leading artistic figure of all time, who wrote and produced holovision plays.

X26 Who was chiefly responsible for the first space colony.

X28 Most responsible for the planetary engineering of Mars into an exhilarating human habitat.

X31 Inventor of a vaccine that protects humans from cancer.

Other future notables are described who developed nano-technology, explained macro-economics in a world of abundance (where three-quarters of the population is retired), wrote the greatest novels, invented personal robots, unified the Arab states into a durable entity, devised practical techniques for cleaning up ocean pollution, became the greatest cook of all time, developed the first usable system for psychokinesis, became the greatest poet ever, developed cryonics for restoring frozen human bodies to health, and captained the first successful interstellar expedition.

Chapter 4

CREATIVITY AS A LIGHT BULB OR MAZE METAPHOR

Stuart Nagel

We have tentatively adopted the policy maze shown in Figure 4-1 as the logo for *Creativity Plus* and for the Creativity Plus Association. The maze is a public policy maze because the entrance is labeled "Policy Problem In," and the exit is labeled "Policy Problem Out." One could also define a public policy maze as one that deals with public policy subject matter.

Figure 4-1. Using A Maze as a Metaphor for Policy Analysis

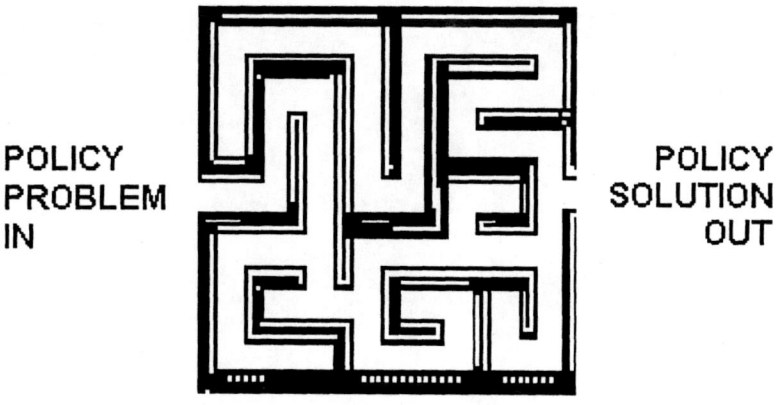

POLICY
PROBLEM
IN

POLICY
SOLUTION
OUT

Systematic Creativity May be the Key
to Solving Policy Problems

This chapter will offer two introductory policy mazes. Future issues of *Creativity Plus* may also contain one or two policy mazes that our readers can try to solve. We will probably just publish one maze at a time, along with the solution to the maze from the previous issue. We are publishing two mazes to begin with to show that it is possible to have a policy maze that deals with one of the six policy fields of economic, technology, social, political, international, and legal policy. We also want to provide a policy maze that deals with one of the four developing regions of Africa, Asia, East Europe, or Latin America.

For a policy field, the next page shows a maze that deals with nuclear-waste dumping. The object is to go from the sign that says "Start at the base of any trial" up to the sign that says "Road." We are rushing up the side of a ravine to block a nuclear-waste truck from getting to the end of the road, where it will then dump its nuclear waste into the ravine. As a hint, this maze involves the principle of Vladimir Lenin and others that it is sometimes necessary to take one step backward in order to take two steps forward. As a further hint, we show which of the five starting trails is likely to be part of the winning route. The solution will be given in the next issue of *Creativity Plus*.

For a developing region, the page after the next page shows the Great Wall of China. The object is to reach Jiang Zemin's tent for a conference without running into an obstruction. Jiang is Secretary-General of the Chinese Communist Party. You can go up and down ladders, but you cannot climb or jump off the wall where there is no ladder. Likewise, you can go through tower openings to proceed from one part of the wall to the next part, but you cannot proceed from one part to the next where the wall is broken. You must also go around rocks, rather than over them, although you can go over ditches. As a hint, we show the beginning part of the route which goes up a ladder through a tower down a ladder and around rocks. This maze also involves taking a step backward in order to achieve the goal. It also involves the policy principle of having a goal or goals to proceed to.

Both these mazes come from the *Great Book of Mazes* by Roger Moreau which was published in 1997 by the Sterling Publishing Company, 387 Park Avenue South, New York, NY 10016. The book contains 320 pages of interesting mazes. A few of them will be used as policy mazes in future issues of *Creativity Plus*. We also welcome mazes submitted by our readers.

Figure 4-2. Stop Nuclear Waste Dumping

These trucks are going to dump radioactive waste into the canyon. Get up the trail in a hurry and stop them. Time is short. Hopefully you will be right the first time.

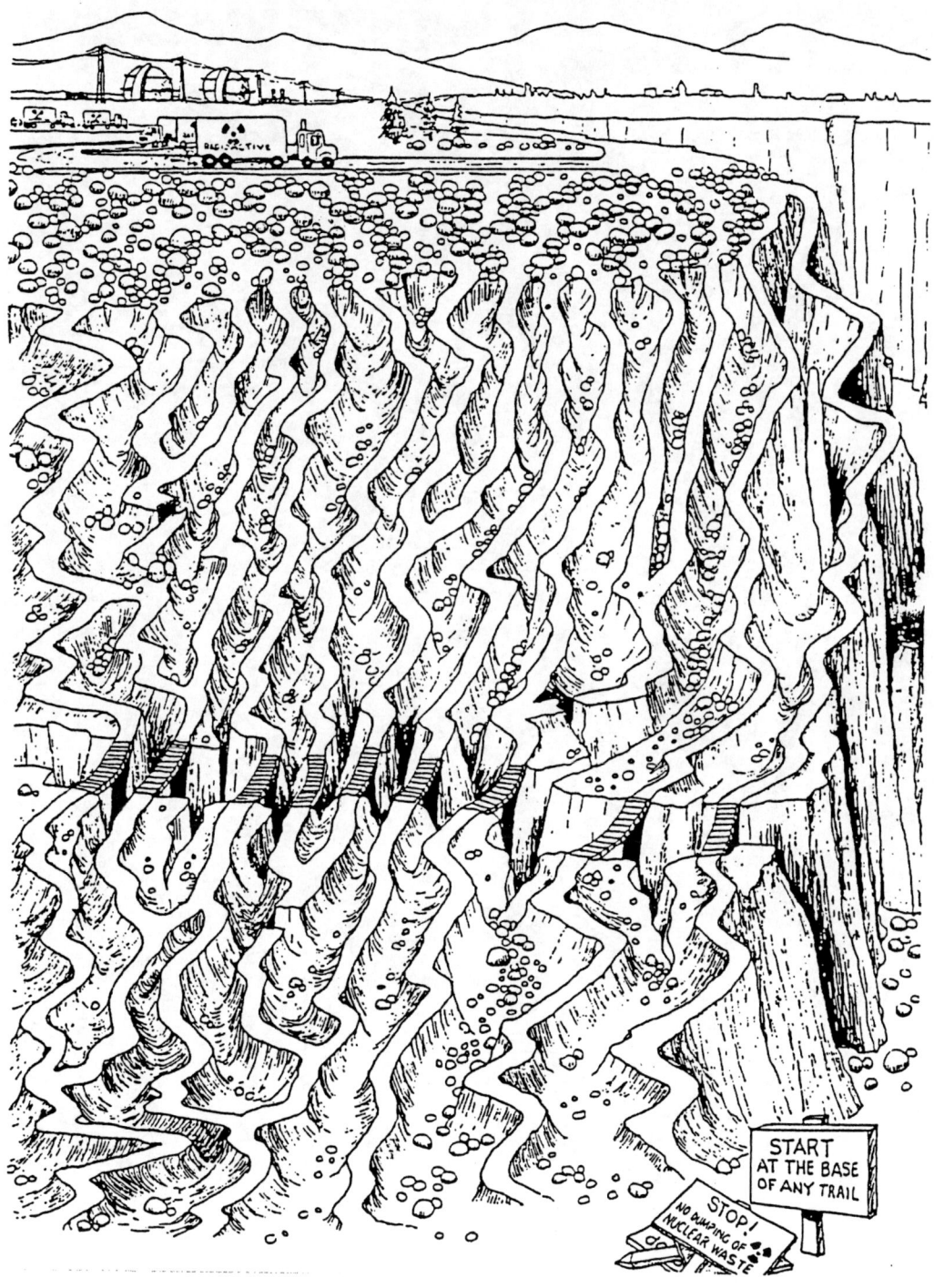

Figure 4-3. The Great Wall of China

To reach Jiang Zemin's tent, navigate a clear path on and around the Great Wall of China by going up and down ladders and through tower openings.

Chapter 5

CREATIVITY AS CAUSE AND EFFECT

Stuart Nagel

This chapter is organized in terms of creativity on a societal level and on an individual level. That is an important distinction which occasionally occurs in *Creativity Plus*. A creative society is one that does a lot of inventing. Likewise a creative individual is one who also does lots of inventing. Inventing in this context means being usefully innovative in solving diverse problems, not necessarily innovative regarding mechanical devices.

The distinction between societal and individual creativity shows up in articles that we have already published. For example, Chapter 10 on "Generating Creative Ideas" in this Handbook emphasizes individual creativity, and Chapter 8 on "Federal Policy" emphasizes societal creativity. Chapter 11 on "Creative Problem Solving" and Chapter 16 "Imagination" emphasize individuals. Chapter 22 on "Win-Win Creativity" and Chapters 23-24 on "Government Innovation" emphasize society.

The distinction may be especially important in talking about the causes and effects of creativity. On the societal level, we are talking about public policy as causes and social change as effects. On the individual level, we are talking about (1) personality characteristics as causes of creativity and (2) benefits and costs to individuals as effects of creativity.

I. THE SOCIETAL LEVEL

A. Creativity as a Cause of Social Changes

Creativity improves every field of public policy and every field of knowledge. The fields of public policy are frequently divided into economic, technology, social, political, international, and legal policies, as indicated in Table 5-1. Those categories also correspond to about six fields of theoretical and practical knowledge including (1) business, (2) science and engineering, (3) social work and education, (4) public administration, (5) diplomacy, trade and technology transfer, and (6) law practice, judging, legislating, and law as a social institution. One could also talk about creativity in art, music, literature, and sports as social institutions.

Perhaps the more interesting aspects of Table 5-1 are the examples used to illustrate the six areas of public policy and societal institutions. All the examples are from the 1990s. They are also highly important showing that creativity is very much with us. Indeed, it may be more with us than at any time in history because creativity grows on prior knowledge of which we have more now than ever before. Each invention tends to generate two or more inventions at a possibly exponential rate until there is a plateauing out.

Thus, innovation tends to occur like a positively-sloped S-curved curve relating time on the horizontal dimension to innovation on the vertical dimension. Such a curve tends to be flat at first and low on innovation, and then it rises with new inventions in the field until it plateaus out at a high level. That does not mean general innovation plateaus out. It means there is eventually a plateauing out regarding new developments of specific inventions like the automobile or the radio. There is, however, an expanding stream of innovation in the realm of transportation, communication, and other basic human activities.

The six specific examples may not be clear from the abbreviations and phrases used. They are:

1. TOTAL QUALITY MANAGEMENT in business with its emphasis on satisfying consumers through low prices and high quality in order to increase market share and profits, as contrasted to trying to maximize profits by increasing prices and decreasing money spent on quality improvements.
2. OFFICE SOFTWARE includes word processing, file management, spreadsheets, and graph drawing software. Such software greatly increases the productivity of people working in offices. Other improvements in computer technology increase the productivity of people working in factories.
3. E-MAIL has revolutionized communication among nations, sellers-buyers, people in the same firm at different locations, research collaborators, and distance teaching. E-mail is also facilitating interaction among family members, doctor-patient relations, relations among legal disputants, and other relations that involve human interaction.

4. THE INVISIBLE INK VOTING refers to the win-win method of voting, first developed in South Africa. It involves multiple voting sites, voting holidays, and on-site registration to facilitate everybody being able to vote easily. At the same time, whenever a person tries to vote, they must put their hand under an ultraviolet light or an infrared light. If no invisible ink shows up, they are allowed to vote. They then dip their hand into a bowl of invisible ink that will show up if they try to vote again within the voting time. Such a system can achieve the conservative goal of preventing double voting (even better than checking signatures), while at the same time achieving the liberal goal of getting everybody to vote (even better than postcards, motor voter, precinct registration, or other relatively ineffective facilitators).

5. THE INTERNATIONAL COMMUNITY is revolutionizing the world by initially eliminating or drastically reducing tariffs and other trade barriers among the members of the community. The community then increases its mutually beneficial effectiveness by facilitating the movement of people and ideas as well as goods. Such communities will eventually cover all regions of the world, and regional communities will join together to form super-regional communities thereby further expanding the benefits. All these examples of creativity may at first work contrary to the interests of those who are dependent on the old ways of doing things, but good public policy facilitates the transition to the new ways on the part of displaced workers and firms.

6. The sixth example under the category of law effects is ADR or ALTERNATIVE DISPUTE RESOLUTION. This movement began as any kind of ad hoc dispute settlement mechanism that was an alternative to going to court. The initial purpose was largely to reduce delay and congestion in the courts. Early ADR or arbitration involved win-lose rules like the courts. The subsequent emphasis has been on mediation, which emphasizes compromises where both sides win on some matters and lose on others. The most recent forms of ADR emphasize win-win mediation or super-optimizing whereby all major sides come out ahead of their best initial expectations. Such a form of ADR may require more creativity than adjudication, arbitration, or traditional mediation does. The more win-win cases we have and the more categories we put them into, the easier it becomes to resolve disputes in a win-win way in the future.

The bottom of Table 5-1 says "Creativity Leads to Societal Improvements." That is generally true. Sometimes, however, an evil person can be creative and develop some thing that worsens some aspect of society. Nevertheless, in the intermediate and long runs, ideas that make for improvements tend to win out in the marketplace of ideas and products, assuming those marketplaces are reasonably free.

Table 5-1. Creativity as a Cause of Social Changes
(What Societal Effects Does Creativity Have?)

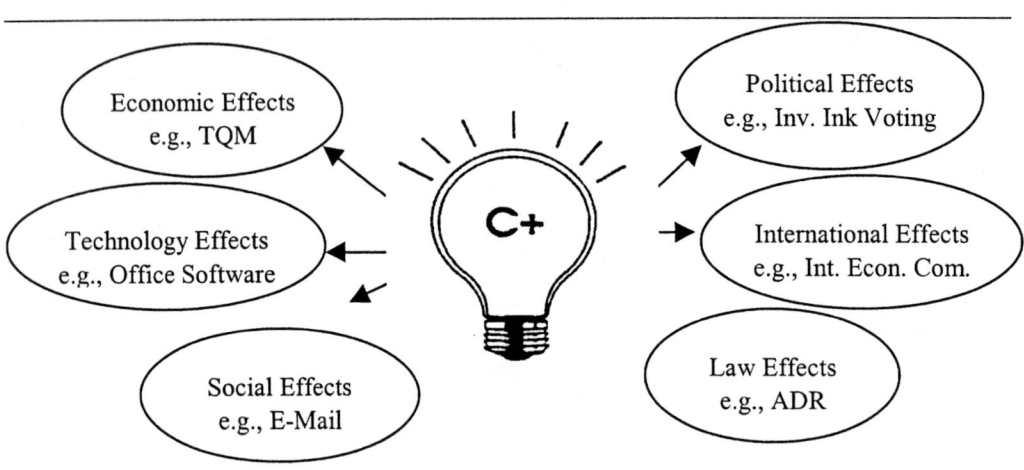

Creativity Leads to Societal Improvements

B. Creativity as an Effect of Public Policies

Table 5-2 shows creativity as being caused by six policy factors or sets of variables in somewhat random order. We could give an example for each of these as we did with effects:

1. For FREE SPEECH, we could show how uncreative the Soviet Union was in dealing with agriculture because of government stifling regarding Stalin's emphasis on environmental rather than genetic determination. We could also use how Hitler stifled creativity regarding the development of the atomic bomb, which they considered based on Jewish physics.

2. EDUCATION AND TRAINING. There we could talk in terms of cultural groups that place a high emphasis on education. We could use that element to help explain Jews and Israelis doing well in terms of Nobel prizes. If getting a university education and becoming a professor is considered so important, then such people are bound to win some Nobel prizes. East Indians are also doing well with computer software, but India has a high rate of illiteracy. It is a split society with many well-educated Ph.D.s (maybe more so per capita than any other country) but at the same time more illiteracy. The explanation may have something to do with urban Indians versus rural Indians.

3. That gets at the next item which is access to LIBRARIES. They are primarily a big city occurrence, although also associated with universities. The Internet is also making library information more widely available. Information is not just in

books. It also comes from interaction with others which may be more likely to occur in cities that in rural areas.

4. LABORATORIES. There are some famous ones in the world that have been conducive to creativity such as the Center for Advanced Study at Princeton or Max Planck Laboratory in Germany. Relevant policy think tanks include the Brookings Institution and the American Enterprise Institute.

5. As for PRESCHOOL SOCIALIZATION that is the subject of an article in the next issue of the *C+ News*.

6. As for REWARDS, they are quite relevant to the articles in the *C+ News*. The next article is one on performance pay as a stimulus to productivity, but also as a stimulus to creativity. That gets into the profit motive. It also gets into the article in the last *C+* issue by William Baumol saying that one of the benefits of competition is inventing new ideas partly in order to receive the reward of making money for what it will buy and its symbolic significance. Jim Clark developed Netscape partly from the stimulus of thinking about what he could develop that would make a billion dollars, rather than starting from the stimulus of what he could develop that would cure AIDS, poverty, or illiteracy.

Table 5-2. Creativity as an Effect of Public Policies (What Policies Cause Creativity?)

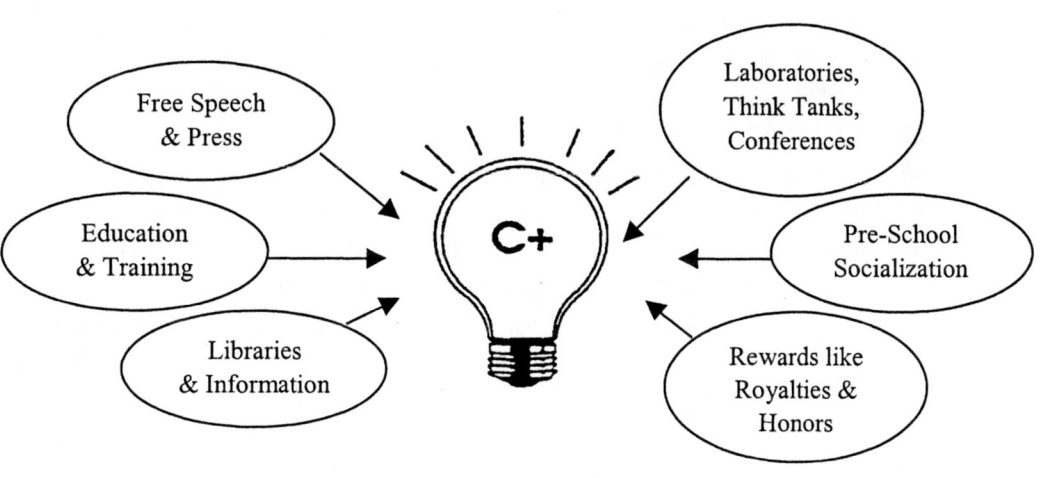

Creativity is Made Not Born

II. The Individual Level

For further details on the individual causes and effects of creativity, see Volume 2, Chapter 13 on "Individual Causes" and Chapter 14 on "Individual Effects."

III. Creativity as an Effect of Useful Tools

This section deals with creativity as an effect of useful tools. One could also say that this section deals with the role of individual facilitators in stimulating creativity. Those facilitators include the following:

1. HOW-TO-DO-IT LISTS. Such lists appear in the such chapters as (1) Chapter 10 on "Generating Creativity Ideas," (2) Chapter 14 on "Sources of Goals, Policies, and Relations," (3) Chapter 11 on "Creative Problem Solving," and (4) Chapter 13 on "Bopping Out of the Box."
2. INSPIRATIONAL AIDS. These include audio and visual aids like those described in Chapter 17 on "Inspirational Aids." To find an ideal combination of audio and visual aids, one can experiment with whatever device is available for sampling video and audio tapes and disks.
3. OTHER PEOPLE. Those people can be pushing, facilitating, or pulling people, as described in Chapter 10 on "Generating Creative Ideas" in this Handbook. They might also be people who are sexually attractive, as described in Chapter 21 on "Creativity and Sex."
4. CREATIVITY AIDING SOFTWARE. The most appropriate software might be spreadsheet-based with goals on the columns, alternatives on the rows, and relations between the alternatives and the goals in the cells. The object is to find an alternative that gets the highest total score on all the goals collectively, on certain goals, or on both the conservative and liberal goals.
5. SLEEP, FOOD, EXERCISE, AND HEALTH AIDS. All in moderation. Too much sleep means missed opportunities to be creative. Too little sleep can interfere with creativity and can even be hallucinatory. Too much food is sleep-producing. Too little food may weaken one's body and mind. Too much exercise can be exhausting. Too little exercise can be stultifying.
6. FLEXIBLE ORGANIZATION. This means developing a reasonably firm schedule of constructive creativity activities, but with flexibility for sleeping, eating, and diversions that generate creativity.

Table 5-3. Creativity as an Effect of Useful Tools

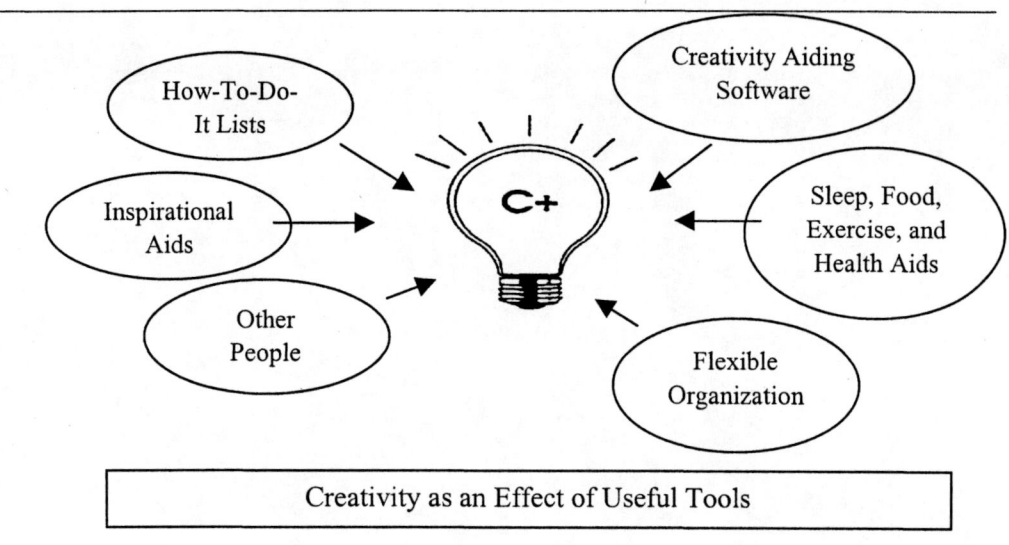

Creativity as an Effect of Useful Tools

PART TWO: PUBLIC POLICY AS A STIMULANT TO CREATIVITY

Chapter 6

CULTIVATION OF CREATIVITY

Harold Lasswell
Yale University

No static certainty is to be found in politics or political science, hence the importance of cultivating an affirmative, inventive, flexible mind. The present chapter treats the cultivation of creativity, since it is concerned with professional training.

In recent decades, the social and behavioral sciences have been able to add precision to the idea of creativity and to identify some of the factors conditioning its incidence. The idea is not a simple one, and many popular connotations are irrelevant. We must, for example, disregard the assumption that whatever is new is creative. Undoubtedly, a novel element is always present. Yet a creative act is not fantastic; it must be able to pass reality tests.

Another erroneous connotation is that creativity is a flash in utter darkness. It is entirely fitting to celebrate the achievements of individuals who give birth to important ideas; it is nonetheless a gross distortion of the creative process to confound it with an individual or with a single moment. The process is social and interactive and, properly understood, reaches forward and backward from the culminating moment. Not every thinker, of course, is able to locate a dramatic instant as Descartes was able to do and to say that his whole theory depended on an "emotional intuition" that struck him on a specific date. Descartes saw his comprehensive vision on the night of November 10, 1619. However, the idea of a rational universe arose and won subsequent ratification in the course of a creative process of great scope and complexity. It is possible for historians of philosophy to identify many influences that played on Descartes and contributed to that heaping up of preconditions to be discovered in all human conduct when closely scrutinized. This is the phenomenon to which Freud referred with the odd but expressive term of "overdetermination." The creative pattern was not complete when Descartes experienced his vision nor even when he committed it to print. Until ratified by others, creativity remains potential; it is not yet actual. The lag may be very long, although in

Descartes' case he carried conviction to enough contemporaries to justify his classification as a creative thinker.

Today we are accustomed to taking the collective character of creativity for granted. We plan inventions. So it was with the atomic bomb; so it is every day in industrial laboratories. When wealth and respect are put at the disposal of persons of recognized skill, they are usually able to gather competent colleagues.

It is, perhaps, pertinent in view of the planned parenthood of ideas in modern society to warn against underestimating the finer structure of creativity. The target is rarely hit by a perfectly straight course. A target can best be described as a working image of a destination which can be reached only by many zig-zags or even returns to the starting point. It is not to be wondered at that the most brilliant results are often, if not, indeed, typically, achieved as side effects rather than as stations along a well-mapped route. In a given research project, the ostensible target may or may not be reached promptly or with much originality; yet society's capital of knowledge continues to grow.

In the physical and biological sciences, the peculiar character of creativity has long been understood. Able research men have learned to proceed in a way that laymen sometimes regard as fraudulent. Capable research workers do not like to tie themselves closely to a single target or to a predescribed method. They want elbow room to explore promising side lanes and to devise new procedures or even to pursue basic scientific ideas at a certain distance. They are concerned that science itself grows only in this fashion; hence they are not true scientists if they bind themselves in advance to a map too precisely drawn. In the budgeting of research, it is therefore taken for granted that the allotment includes a margin of support for general exploration. Since the repertory of modern science is enormous, many research implications invariably appear once capable investigators get to work on any concrete task.

Given these facts, it seems defensible to obtain research funds in the name of popular problems, while keeping free of any inner commitment of public pledge to solve the problem at once. Consider the notorious case of cancer. As of this moment, the millions of dollars and man hours of talent that have gone into cancer research have fallen short of the goal. Research in the name of cancer is nearly as permissive as the pursuit of truth itself. Yet the whole episode is not to be dismissed as a plot by research administrators engaged in building rival empires at the expense of a credulous public. The by-products of research launched in the name of cancer are of undoubted importance in many fields. Of this, both research administrators and the beneficiary scientists have been morally certain all the time. And many laymen who join in money-raising share the viewpoint of the scientists, since they know enough science themselves or have had enough experience with good scientists to recognize the policies that are most likely to keep them productive.

The contrast with the typical research situation of political and social scientists is evident. Even rather capable political scientists have rarely had enough self-confidence to adopt the approach that is usual for colleagues in the physical and biological sciences. Hence, their research projects tend to be cut and dried, with deadlines, contents, and procedures rather clearly specified in advance. They typically provide little leeway for the pursuit of promising theoretical leads or for the invention of novel methods.

What can be said when we sum up the fundamental criteria of creativity? An important clue has come from the psychologists of perception. We are not far wrong in condensing the fundamental point into the phrase "context completion." To a degree, context completion is inseparable from any living organism, since life perpetually seeks solutions to the problems of the new environment.

There are vast differences between mild exercises of ingenuity and the masterpieces that are commonly viewed as turning points in the history of thought. What are the distinguishing marks of a contribution, such as those of Planck or Einstein, that receive universal acclaim from knowledgeable scientists? These celebrated instances of intellectual achievement introduced a coherent picture where the conventional map was full of contradiction, confusion, and ambiguity. New ways of looking at the world disclosed a comprehensible pattern in which ancient incompatibilities were redefined and disappeared.

I comment briefly in this connection on the work of a distinguished physician who has influenced political science and many other fields of thought. Sigmund Freud was trained in neurology and cognate disciplines. He was, in fact, reared in one of the most orthodox temples of the "scientism" of the day. All brain functions were to be reduced to objective events. Any mention of subjectivity was seen as a regrettable concession to the undeveloped state of the science.

In his training, Freud was also exposed to contradictory images of reality. For instance, he visited a clinic where the therapeutic efficacy of hypnotism was being demonstrated. Hypnotism obviously relies on communication in a social context to affect inner life and outer conduct. Neither neurons nor chemicals enter visibly into the chain of events that initiates response.

It was not possible for Freud to eliminate the mind-body problem. He nonetheless provided a map in which many hitherto-disjointed observations became intelligible. Without constructing "neural myths" to add to "myths of subjectivity," Freud suggested how human organisms can influence one another. He appeared to treat "instincts" as part of the "body." However, the "soma" was shown to be affected by nonphysical events--in a word, by signs and symbols. The "unconscious" became a patterned repository of primitive instincts as modified by interactions in the social process.

When we examine creativity directly in political science it is soon apparent that context completion is a serviceable guide. The images entertained by those who participate in a political process are conventionally a blend of prescriptions and observed "facts of life." Almost every serious, competent study in political science redefines a conventional image and refocuses the connection between "preferred norms" and "factual norms."

We have referred to Beard's analysis of economic factors in the forming and ratification of the United States Constitution; it is unquestionably a case in point. A monument of the same kind is Michels' study of social-democratic parties in Europe. The social-democratic elites were accustomed to speaking in the name of democracy. Michels drew attention to the facts that the leaders tended to stay in office for many years and that in many cases their children succeeded them in office. He summed up the data by generalizing about the "oligarchical tendencies" of mass political parties. In the long run, it may be that the criteria of oligarchy applied by Michels are too loose to satisfy professional opinion and that he was vague about factors that might reverse a trend toward narrowly held power. Nevertheless, the study was sufficiently compelling to induce great defensiveness and some insight into European socialists of the time.

Few scholars would deny that Marx and Engels were the most original and also most successful political and social theorists of recent generations. If the criteria were changed by de-emphasizing success, a strong case could be made for the opinion that some French thinkers--Saint-Simon, for example--were more inventive or that Bentham is ultimately to be regarded as more creative. For present purposes, it is enough to say that Marx provided the most comprehensive and upsetting confrontation of conventional imagery on record. He provided rebellion with the favorite intellectual tool of the status quo, namely, history. Rebellion was no longer perceived as personal caprice, disorder, or heroism, but as a transpersonal natural law of society that could be grasped by an instructed mind trained in the necessary method of thought. Hence, the triumph of realistic thinking was not to "make" history but to harmonize with reality, rebellion became the ultimate conformity.

The capture of the appeal to history is correctly interpreted as an impressive burst of creativity; it is of particular interest because it exemplifies "rejection by partial incorporation" of an "enemy" ideology and also provides a case of differentiation by an appeal to method.

The first point--the use of partial incorporation--means that a mode of justification, the appeal to history, was taken over by Marx and Engels, although most of the doctrines asserted in the ideology of the social order that "history" originally justified were in fact rejected. Socialism in turn often became the target of a comparable strategy, notably when Hitler opposed "international" socialism in the name of "nation" and "race."

The second point--differentiation by an appeal to method--received tremendous emphasis in the Marx-Engels contribution as a means of borrowing the prestige of the physical sciences and transferring it to a counter-ideological system. "Historical materialism" was put forward as a procedure by which the attention of an individual could focus on data revealing the dynamic and implacable sequence of history from feudalism through capitalism to the classless society. When French revolutionary thinkers assailed feudalism, they also appealed to method, namely, the test of "reason." But the connotations of the term were capricious. My reason may lead to affirmations which your reason is unwilling to accept. By the time Marx and Engels wrote, a more disciplined idea of method had become recognized. The conception of universal law validated by empirical observation seemed to provide a tool for controlling the ebullience of individual subjectivity. "Historical materialism" revived the notion of inescapable truth ascertainable by proper method.

These examples of creativity enable us to pose our present problem in fundamental terms. How can we strengthen the probability that future questions will be approached with the balance between innovation and realism that characterizes high-level creativity?

For years to come, the principal responsibility for professional preparation and hence for the cultivation of creativity will presumably lie with graduate departments of universities. It will continue to be the task of such academic structures to offer the basic introduction to scope and methods and to arrange the environment of graduate students in harmony with the requirements of professional objectives. It is, after all, the graduate department that consolidates rival conceptions of the profession into working unity.

How does a graduate department sustain the creativity of professors and students? Experience shows how rarely any department succeeds in maintaining its position as a well-balanced representative of the past and as a pioneer.

Part of the difficulty comes form the fact that, in an epoch of accelerating change, the training that fits men for today may unfit them for tomorrow. At any given time, the leading figures are somewhat obsolete. At best, they provide partial models for the problem-solvers who will be best adapted to the tasks of the next thirty of forty years. We must suggest, I think, that a factor in support of a creative department is an acute sense of partial obsolescence.

The versatility and competence with which political scientists cope with the future depend in no small degree on professional preparation. From the beginning of their specialized studies the larger context must be kept in sight if the perspectives conducive to creativity are to be nourished and applied. Hence, the basic orientation to the scope and methods of political science is of strategic importance. Properly conceived, introductory exercises in "Scope and Method" are returned to throughout the years of professional preparation and continue to challenge, guide, and inspire the political scientist at every subsequent phase of his career.

NOTES

1. Harold Lasswell died in about 1975. He was one of the founders of the Policy Studies Organization. This paper was based on a speech at the University of Maryland. It does not seem to have been previously published.

Chapter 7

POLITICAL, ECONOMIC, AND SOCIAL-PSYCHOLOGICAL STIMULATORS

Stuart Nagel

The following political, economic, sociological, and psychological institutions or ways of doing things in a society are conducive to innovative and effective public policy-making. This includes public policies that can enable conservatives, liberals, and other major viewpoints to all come out ahead of their best initial expectations simultaneously.

I. POLITICAL METHODS

A. Competitive Political Parties

This is a key facilitator since the out-party is constantly trying to develop policies (including possibly SOS policies) in order to become the in-party. The in-party is also busy developing new policies in order to stay the in-party. New policies are developed largely as a result of changing domestic and international conditions, not just for the sake of newness. Without the stimulus of an out-party, the in-party would have substantially less incentive to be innovative. More important, without the possibility of becoming the in-party, the out-party would lose its incentive to be innovative. More innovation generally comes from the out-party than the in-party (all other factors held constant), including the possibility of SOS innovations.

B. Better Policy Analysis Methods and Institutions

SOS solutions are likely to be facilitated by policy analysis methods that deal with multiple goals, multiple alternatives, missing information, spreadsheet based decision-aiding software, and a concern for successful adoption and implementation. Better policy analysis institutions refer to training, research, funding, publishing, and networking associations. These institutions can be part of the activities of universities, government agencies, and independent institutes in the private sector. The extent to which these policy institutions deal with super-optimizing analysis will make them even more relevant to facilitating SOS solutions.

II. ECONOMIC POLICIES

A. Competitive Business Firms

Competition among political parties may be essential for facilitating SOS public policy. Competition among business firms may be essential for facilitating a prosperous economy and a prosperous world through international business competition. Numerous examples can be given of nations that failed to advance and collapsed due largely to a one-party system, such as the former Soviet Union. Likewise, numerous examples can be given of business firms that failed to advance and virtually collapsed due largely to lack of substantial competition such as the American steel industry. The American automobile industry has not collapsed, but it did fail to develop small cars, cars that resist style changes, safer cars, less expensive cars, and more durable cars in comparison to the international competition that was not taken seriously until almost too late.

B. Well-Targeted Subsidies and Tax Breaks

In the context of super-optimum solutions, this tends to mean subsidies and tax breaks that increase national productivity and international competitiveness. Such subsidies and tax breaks are the opposite of handouts that provide a disincentive to increased productivity on the part of either welfare recipients or big business. Good targeting in this regard especially refers to upgrading skills and stimulating technological innovation and diffusion. A dollar invested in those kinds of subsidies is likely to pay off many times over without necessarily having to wait very long for the results.

C. Increased National Productivity

All these facilitators are important. Economists might rightfully consider increased national productivity to be especially important. It leads to an increased gross national product or national income, which means an increased tax base to which the tax rate is applied. If increased productivity increases the tax base, then tax rates can be lowered and still produce more tax money for well-targeted subsidies that produce further increases in national productivity. These increases, however, are not an end in themselves. The increased national income can facilitate finding and implementing SOS solutions that relate to employment, inflation, agriculture, labor, business, poverty, discrimination, education, families, the environment, housing, transportation, energy, health, technological innovation, government structures, government processes, world peace, international trade, and every other public policy field. In other words, with more money and resources available, SOS solutions are facilitated, but SOS solutions often draw upon creativity that is associated with doing much better on relevant goals with constant or decreasing resources.

III. SOCIOLOGY: CHILDHOOD SOCIALIZATION

Risk takers get generated from about age 0 to 5 in little children depending on whether they are allowed to take chances or treated in such a way that they never come in contact with anything that might hurt them. There is certainly a need for encouraging more experimentation on the part of children within reason. More rebelliousness, more of the kind of trying out to see what will happen if you push your food off the highchair onto the floor without being punished for doing so, to see if the bowl will break or not. That does not necessarily mean that you jump off the third story porch to see if your head will break.

Liberals have a lot of trouble talking about socialization because it sounds like brainwashing people. It can be done in a brainwashing way, or it can be done in a way that encourages children to think things out for themselves to some extent. An example might be telling children not to discriminate on the basis of race or gender, as contrasted to setting up a situation where they more creatively reason that discrimination is undesirable. Such a situation might involve the teacher calling for volunteers to erase the blackboard and virtually everyone volunteers. The teacher says we cannot have so many people erasing the blackboard, and we might therefore just pick the black girls. She then asks for reactions and alternative suggestion. She thereby stimulates creativity and possibly an implicit understanding of such concepts as merit treatment, sharing benefits, sharing costs, having a minimum benefit threshold, having a maximum cost threshold, and other such ideas without using those words.

IV. PSYCHOLOGY OF SOS SOLUTIONS

A. Innovative Risk Taking

This is an important SOS facilitator because many SOS solutions involve technological fixes. In order to develop new technologies, many people usually had to risk substantial amounts of money, time, effort, and other resources. There may have been a strong possibility that it would have all been wasted. An SOS society needs more people who are willing to take such chances. Classic examples include Marie and Pierre Curie who sacrificed about 30 years of work plus their health to develop radium and thus radioactivity, which is part of the basis for nuclear energy. Thomas Edison frequently not only risked his resources but his whole reputation by announcing inventions before he had developed them in order to give himself an ego risk as a stimulus to quickly inventing what he falsely said he had already done.

B. Sensitivity to Opporunity Costs

This means either through socialization or an appropriate incentive structure trying to get decision-makers to be more sensitive to the mistake of failing to try out a new idea that might work wonders, as contrasted to being so sensitive to sins of commission rather than omission. Both wrongs are undesirable. One can, however, say that a police officer who wrongly beats a suspect is doing less harm to society than a president who wrongly fails to adopt a new health care program that could save numerous lives or a new education program that could greatly improve productivity and the quality of life. A person who is sensitive to opportunity costs tends to say "nothing ventured, nothing gained," whereas an insensitive person tends to say "nothing ventured, nothing lost." We need more of the former in order to facilitate the generating, adopting, and implementing of SOS solutions.

C. SOS Combination of Pessimism and Optimism

This does not mean a balance or a compromise between being pessimistic and being optimistic. It means being 100% pessimistic or close to it regarding how bad things are and how much worse they are going to get unless we actively do something about them including developing SOS solutions. It simultaneously means being 100% optimistic or close to it regarding how good things can get in the future if we vigorously work at them including developing SOS solutions This is in contrast to those who say the present is wonderful and needs little improvement. It is also in contrast to those who say the present may be wonderful or not so wonderful but some invisible hands or automatic forces of Adam Smith, Karl Marx, or God will automatically improve the future.

D. Constantly Seeking Higher Goals

This list of social facilitators is in random order. Some of the items overlap or interact, but it is better to overlap than leave gaps in this context. It is appropriate perhaps to have the last facilitator relate to constantly seeking higher goals. Traditional goal-seeking leads to compromises. Worse, it can lead to one side trying to win 100% and the other side losing 100%, but the war, strike, litigation, or other negative dispute resolution leads to both sides losing close to 100%. Obviously seeking higher goals is more likely to result in higher goal achievement than seeking lower goals, including SOS goal achievement. The counter argument sometimes made is that higher goals lead to frustration because of the gap between goals and achievement. There may be more frustration in fully achieving low goals that provide a low quality of life when others are doing better. High societal goal-seeking (including SOS solutions) is facilitated by all of the above factors, but it is a factor in itself because high goal-seeking tends to become a self-fulfilling prophecy.

NOTES

1. From S. Nagel, *Creativity: Being Usefully Innovative in Solving Diverse Problems* (Ashgate Publishers, 1999).
2. From S. Nagel, *Super-Optimum Solutions and Win-Win Policy: Basic Concepts and Principles* (Quorum-Greenwood, 1997), 58-68.

Chapter 8

COMPETITION AND INNOVATION

Michael Weinstein
New York Times
William Baumol
New York University

Capitalism, every undergraduate student of economics learns, thrives on competition. The brilliant virtue of the invisible hand of competition is that it forces firms to reduce costs, cut prices and thereby enrich consumers. This engaging tale has buttressed every economics narrative since Adam Smith lucidly explained 200 years ago how competition channels the natural greed of individuals into serving the social good.

Now William Baumol, an economics professor at New York University, wants to rewrite the basic tale. Yes, competition creates wealth. But in his new formulation, price cutting becomes a sideshow. Innovation takes center stage as the "primary weapon of competition." And the key to innovation is a clever form of collaboration among rivals.

Innovation, the process of translating inventions and new ideas into commercial products, is largely responsible for the tenfold rise in the living standards of American families over the last 100 years, he says in a new manuscript. Mr. Baumol's contribution is not to emphasize the impact of innovation but to pinpoint how competition forces companies to make innovation routine, much as marketing and advertising are.

Capitalism, in Mr. Baumol's analysis, emerges as a system that hums because it has figured out how to make innovation humdrum.

Mr. Baumol shows how companies pour money not only into their own research and development but also into such operations by their rivals. Yes, their rivals. Firms participate in joint ventures that hire teams of researchers to develop technologies that the firms will share. They also engage in the largely unrecognized practice by which companies enter into technology-sharing compacts. Under these compacts, a company like IBM writes contracts with competitors, like Hitachi. The companies promise to license future innovations to each other for a set fee. That way if Hitachi comes up with a spiffy next-generation disk drive, IBM is guaranteed the right to incorporate Hitachi's new drive in its own computers.

It might seem odd for an economist like Mr. Baumol to herald collaboration among potential competitors. By jumping into the arms of rivals, companies appear to dull their incentive to innovate on their own. After all, if they can imitate rivals, why bother to innovate on one's own?

To understand Mr. Baumol's point, put yourself in the place of IBM. You could try to piggyback off Hitachi's innovations, dismissing your own engineers. But that strategy would collapse. At the very least, you would be dishing out hundreds of millions of dollars each year to rivals without getting anything in return. Worse, Hitachi would soon drop the agreements, because they make sense only if it expects to get about as many new products from IBM as it provides to IBM.

Nor would it make economic sense to beef up your investment in innovations without entering technology-sharing contracts. If four or five of your major rivals share innovations among themselves, then they will generate lots of ideas, drowning out the efforts of your one research department. And anything you don't figure out on your own will be offered to consumers by all your rivals. You simply cannot afford to bear that risk. The compacts eliminate the threat that a misstep in the technology race will drive you out of business. Besides, Mr. Baumol says, the compacts generate licensing fees that have become "a substantial business activity in itself."

Mr. Baumol's analysis makes a bigger point, far beyond the benefits and costs to individual companies. Technology-sharing contracts also help the economy--that is to say consumers--by spreading the benefit of innovation far beyond the customers of any one company. You don't have to buy from Hitachi to get the benefit of its breakthroughs.

Drawing on his career as a consultant as well as scholar, Mr. Baumol says "that of the 20 or so firms that engage in substantial research and development for whom I have consulted over the past few years, almost all had technology-sharing agreements of one sort or another with other firms in their industries." The managers of these companies, he says, often agreed to them reluctantly. But the scientists, especially the engineers, often required them as a condition of their employment: they simply refused to work for a company that would not allow them to communicate with their peers.

He points to a compact that the Perkin-Elmer Corporation, which sells scientific instruments using precision optics, has had with Hitachi for the right to license innovations that either company might adopt. Under the compact, each company provides a menu of innovations under development, any of which it promises to make available for a fee that often ranges from 6 to 7.5 percent of the price of the product that incorporates the innovation. Perkin-Elmer has entered about 100 other compacts since World War II. United Technologies' Pratt & Whitney, a manufacturer of aircraft jet engines, has technology-sharing agreements with a rival, General Electric.

The computer industry, Mr. Baumol says, is littered with technology-sharing agreements. Mr. Baumol's point is that innovations are no longer left to historical quirk or random feats of genius. Rather competition has forced corporations to bring to market a steady diet of innovative products from their own scientists or, if not, from scientists working for their competitors.

Mr. Baumol's focus on innovation may not seem novel. Joseph Schumpeter and others made it the core of their theories of economic progress. But in fact, the Baumol formulation overturns the thrust of modern textbooks.

The typical (dreary?) presentation starts with chapter after chapter about how upward sloping supply curves and downward sloping demand curves interact in idealized markets to determine prices. When all goes well, market prices produce efficiency, a wondrous social outcome whereby the economy churns out the most output possible with its limited amounts of labor, land and machinery. Nothing goes to waste.

But market prices do not produce wondrous results in the presence of imperfections like monopolies. One imperfection, called an externality, is crucial to understanding the important message of the Baumol manuscript. Markets go haywire when the impact of a trade between buyer and seller extends beyond the two parties directly involved.

Take innovation. The profit from innovation routinely leaks to third parties. A firm spends a lot of money bringing to market a clever new electronic organizer or tennis racket. Ten nanoseconds later, another firm tears the product apart and reverse engineers a variation that gets around the patent. So the first firm winds up making relatively little money, a heavy disincentive for would-be entrepreneurs.

Professor Edward Wolff, a colleague of Mr. Baumol at New York University, estimates that innovators can expect to earn about 10 cents a year from each dollar they invest. But because the innovation leaks to other companies and other sectors, the economy as a whole reaps a benefit of about 50 cents. The implication, according to the textbooks, is that capitalism provides entrepreneurs too little of the profit that their investments create for the economy. So they invest too little in the development of products. Consumers suffer from high prices, restricted choice and delayed innovation.

The traditional analysis, then, says that capitalism blunders at generating innovation over the long run. Mr. Baumol's manuscript reverses this presumption. Competition forces firms to innovate, engaging in what Mr. Baumol says "is tantamount to a technology arms race." The technology-sharing compacts, by generating a steady flow of licensing fees for IBM, Perkin-Elmer and other innovators, turn innovation into a routine profit-making activity. The competitive system, he says, goes "a long way, perhaps all the way, toward generating the right amount of innovation." The compacts overcome leakage by putting more of the economy's gains from innovation into the bank accounts of the innovators.

By reducing the risk of innovation (a company that goes down the wrong technological road can lease the innovations it did not come up with) and increasing revenues, technology-sharing compacts make innovation profitable, routine and plentiful. As proof, he points to nonmarket societies that generated plenty of inventions but few applications. Medieval China, for example, invented gunpowder, paper, the printing press and probably the compass and the water wheel. But these inventions failed to raise living standards until adapted into consumer products by societies that were less hostile to commerce. The genius of Western capitalism was to translate invention into the goods and services that enrich everyday life.

Mr. Baumol tells a tale rich in details about the market's use of collaboration to overcome problems of innovation. Along the way he turns standard analysis upside down. Textbooks congratulate markets for their short-run efficiency, even though Mr. Baumol says the short run is nothing spectacular. Entrenched monopolies, labor-market rigidities, perverse management incentives and many other problems are pervasive. The standard analysis goes on to criticize the market for shortchanging innovation and growth, even though "spectacular growth is the market's outstanding accomplishment."

NOTES

1. From *New York Times*. June 7. 1999

Chapter 9

FEDERAL POLICY

J. David Roessner
Georgia Tech University

I. FEDERAL AND NON-FEDERAL INTERVENTION

The federal government's interest in the diffusion of innovations, viewed instrumentally, focuses on efforts to introduce policy- and technological-innovations deemed beneficial into the economy and political system earlier – and speed their diffusion more rapidly – than would occur under "normal market conditions," and to slow down or halt the diffusion of innovations deemed harmful. There are several ways in which federal intervention in the non-federal sector can be rationalized. In the case of private industry, the rationale involves a variant of the market imperfection argument often used to justify federal expenditures for research and development (R&D). For example, intervention is justified when individual adopters cannot capture sufficient benefits of the innovation to warrant adoption, yet widespread use of the innovation would produce substantial social benefits to the nation. In the private sector, federal diffusion-related activities take forms such as: efforts to commercialize the products of federally sponsored R&D (e.g., NASA spinoffs, nuclear reactors) and speeding the rate of diffusion of innovations having large social benefits (e.g., automobile seat belts, energy conserving technologies, cancer chemotherapeutic compounds). Several strategies can be employed by federal agencies interested in diffusing innovations to or via industry. These include demonstrations, subsidies to purchasers, market analyses, technical assistance to purchasers, regulation, and legislation.

In the non-federal public sector (state and local governments, primarily), the rationale for intervention is a combination of historical, political, and economic factors. These include, first, the effort to maximize the application of federal R&D to public problems. This is often expressed by the phrase "if we can go to the moon, surely we can..." Second, state and local governments have assumed an increased burden for planning and resource allocation decision-making due to federal programs such as general revenue sharing (and its consequent devolution of decision-making), implementation of federal categorical grant programs, and a shift of the public focus from "national" concerns such as equality of opportunity to more localized concerns such as crime, transportation, pollution, and education. Third, many perceive a need to stimulate change in a sector commonly believed to be resistant to innovation, yet in need of changes that would increase the efficiency and quality of services delivered. The focus in this article is on federal policy and the stimulation of innovation adoption among public organizations, especially state and local agencies.

II. QUESTIONS TO ASK

The first question in policy analysis is: Is there a problem? The second is: If there is a problem, what is it? What evidence do we have that there is a problem in the non-federal public sector? There is empirical evidence of low productivity growth in the public sector relative to industry. Some theories suggest that this low productivity may be endemic to the public sector. Severe financial problems continue to plague cities, particularly large cities. The federal government has attempted to assist cities and states by conducting research and development intended to be relevant to their problems. Agencies engaged in civilian sector R&D, now approximately $8 billion a year, include the departments of Health, Education & Welfare, Transportation, Housing and Urban Development, and Justice (especially the Law Enforcement Assistance Administration). In addition, agencies operate programs to disseminate knowledge and techniques and provide technical assistance to state and local governments. However, there is evidence that few of these efforts have been successful, or at least as successful as the program designers had intended. Studies have suggested that demonstration programs launched by federal agencies have not in general succeeded in disseminating the products of federal R&D. There continue to be complaints from state and local officials concerning the relevance of the products of federally supported R&D to state and local problems. The Congress has made pronouncements, particularly in legislation establishing the Office of Science and Technology Policy, that register these complaints in a formal way.

There does, then, seem to be a problem. What is it? Some suggest that it is a demand problem in that public organizations, particularly state and local agencies, are inherently less innovative than private ones. Economic theory suggests that the absence of competition leads to a lack of incentives to innovate in such organizations. Organization theory suggests that bureaucracy is designed to conduct routine tasks, not innovative ones. Political scientists point to legal and institutional constraints on public officials' behavior that inhibit innovation. But, are things really as bad as available evidence suggests? Sometimes public agencies get labeled as backward when they fail to adopt a new idea, new technique, or new piece of hardware. But recent studies of innovation decisions in state and local agencies suggest that common needs rarely exist across city and state agencies. The rejection of a new technology might well be rational from the local perspective, despite objective measures of "need" and technological performance.

Moreover, public agencies must be responsive to a much wider range of values than performance: they must be responsive, they must be equitable, they must be open, they must be accountable. A study of the diffusion of 43 technological innovations among 810 cities of 25,000 population and above found that the rates of diffusion were similar to those observed in the diffusion of innovations among private firms. Another study compared rates of innovation diffusion across public and private hospitals and found no clear pattern. These and other findings suggest that there is no obvious basis for assuming that incentives to adopt new technology in the public sector are less than in the private sector.

Nevertheless, it is clear that several institutional features unique to state and local agencies generally act to inhibit innovation by public officials. First, our democratic system requires that agencies be accountable to clients, to legislatures, and to higher levels of government. This means that members of local agencies have multiple appeal routes if a decision from above is not to their liking. In effect, independent actions are extremely difficult to bring about in local government – it is simply hard to get anything done. Second, there are frequent top leadership changes in local government. This leads to short-run thinking and an emphasis on highly visible projects that do not involve high risk. Third, public agencies are responsible to a heterogeneous clientele, a clientele exhibiting a wide range of values. Almost no individual decision to adopt a major innovation (or do anything else significant) is likely to be acceptable to a large majority of any agency's clientele. Finally, public agency outputs are not evaluated in external markets. This means it is difficult to devise performance-related incentives that could lead to improvements in bureaucratic efficiency and effectiveness.

III. New Innovative Research

I should mention that there is some new, exciting research relevant to these problems. This research, which focuses on the incentives and value systems of public officials in state and local governments as they face decisions on whether or not to adopt innovations, has suggested that there may be two separate and independent processes of innovation. One is driven by the need for social approval and peer acceptance among local officials, the other by a sense of professionalism, interest in organizational performance, and the quality of service delivery. If it were possible to specify the conditions under which social approval incentives are dominant relative to performance-related incentives, and vice versa, federal agency strategies for the diffusion of different innovations could clearly reflect these different incentives.

I have suggested that there may be a demand problem, but it may be a problem more of local officials' actual needs and conditions failing to coincide with the characteristics of innovations offered than of bureaucratic inertia. Thus there may also be a supply problem. That is, those organizations and institutions that supply innovations to state and local government may provide inappropriate innovations or an insufficient number of innovations. Several studies have addressed this question; three in particular are pertinent. One is of the fire services, a second focused on the law enforcement R&D

system, and a third dealt with firms in Pennsylvania's Delaware valley near Philadelphia. To summarize briefly, these studies discovered that, in general, firms that supply the state and local market are small and financially weak. They conduct little R&D on their own. New products in the service areas served by these firms often result from "invasion" or spin-off from other companies whose primary market is in the private sector. Finally, the state and local government market is small and generally disaggregated, though these characteristics probably vary widely across service areas. But some firms clearly make it: they successfully produce and market new products to state and local agencies. We do not know very much about the reasons for these firms' success--the kinds of market strategies they employ, or the incentives that other firms have to enter the state and local market. A study has just been initiated, supported by the National Science Foundation, at Syracuse University's School of Management in conjunction with the Syracuse Research Corporation. This study focuses on what are called "urban-oriented industries" and should provide us with an initial, systematic look at the nature and activities of the industries that serve the state and local market.

IV. THE INFRASTRUCTURE PROBLEM

A third explanation for the problem of state and local government innovation involves reference to what might be called the infrastructure problem. In this case demand exists and suppliers are willing to meet it, but communication channels do not exist between suppliers and buyers or among buyers. Here the roles of change agents, intermediary organizations, and other kinds of broker organizations emerge as important. In addition, the roles of informal networks, the grapevine, and other types of communications systems become extremely important. The importance in state and local innovation "systems" of professional associations and standards organizations has been documented in a number of studies. Also documented are wide variations in the degree of integration of these networks across different local government service areas. For example, one observes in the area of transportation a tightly integrated highly technical and effective system of information exchange. In newer areas less blessed by federal funding, one sees a much less integrated and less research-intensive set of organizations. Examples of such situations include air pollution and urban mass transit. While studies of these intermediaries (i.e., professional associations and public interest groups) are continuing, it is clear that state and local officials need credible sources of technical information, particularly information that provides evaluative data on new technology. The federal government and federal agencies are not perceived by state and local agencies as being particularly credible sources of such information.

V. CONCLUSIONS

Several tentative conclusions and suggestions for federal policy can be drawn from the findings of the studies referred to above. Where possible, federal agencies and federal policy makers should avoid pushing particular solutions, that is, technologies, techniques, or systems and ideas. Instead, they should provide resources that could increase the capability of state and local government agencies to identify their own problems, seek and evaluate potential solutions to those problems, and successfully implement the solutions chosen. Second, agencies should employ what might be called "natural points of entry" to accomplish this capacity building goal. Natural points of entry are the existing incentive systems that characterize the environment of local officials, the communications channels in which they are situated, the group of peer professionals to which they are responsive, and the professional values to which they ascribe. Other natural points of entry include training program curricula and tests required for advancement within the civil bureaucracy. Third, if agencies by mandate or inclination must attempt to diffuse particular innovations, they should focus on the process by which they select projects and, in particular, on the role that market information plays at early stages in that process. As part of that market information, agencies need to learn the details of the innovation system of their intended clients: the incentives that motivate suppliers, buyers, regulators, and intermediaries, and the characteristics of the communications channels that link them.

To sum up, there is considerable interest among federal officials in encouraging the diffusion of policy- and technological-innovations. But to be relevant to this interest, future diffusion research must incorporate many more features of diffusion milieus than characteristically has been the case. These features include the nature of demands for change, the activities of suppliers, and the characteristics of the knowledge infrastructure which affect the search for alternative solutions to problems. Diffusion researchers, it would appear, must be modest in their claims that policy-relevant information can be derived from current knowledge about the factors that affect the diffusion of innovations.

PART THREE: HOW TO DO IT LISTS

Chapter 10

GENERATING CREATIVE IDEAS

Stuart Nagel

Perhaps the most useful human skill is the ability to generate creative ideas. It is a skill that cuts across all personal, business, intellectual, public policy, and other problems. It is the kind of skill that on a high level wins Nobel prizes and places in history. On a lower level, it can be useful in naming a dog food, talking one's way out of a traffic ticket, or drafting a well-drafted letter.

There is no article that can guarantee substantial increases in creativity. This article can, however, provide checklists of ideas that may stimulate greater creativity than one might otherwise have.

A useful way of organizing ideas for stimulating creativity is in terms of pushing factors, facilitators, and pulling factors. That three-part organization comes from Frederick Jackson Turner's analysis of the causes of people moving west in the 1800's. The pushing factors included undesirable aspects of the East, such as overcrowding, lack of jobs, and debts. Facilitating factors included wagon trails, railroads, river systems, and other means of transportation. Pulling factors included attractions in the West, such as free land and business opportunities.

In this context, the pushing factors include other people and commitments. The facilitators include relevant literature, working style, and multi-criteria decision-making. The pulling factors include the rewards that go to successful imagination. The rewards here emphasize intellectual rewards partly because the article is based on experience in academic and government activities where monetary rewards are not as great as they are in business. The reader can adjust the ideas, however, to fit other contexts besides the academic and governmental contexts.

I. Pushing Factors

A. Other People as Pushing Factors

Talk with someone else about generating alternatives. Trying to explain alternative ways of achieving something with an audience listening stimulates more ideas than either talking or thinking to one's self. Put one's head together with someone else who is trying to come up with ideas. The interaction of two or more people trying to generate ideas tends to work better than one person alone. Have contact with stimulating colleagues via correspondence, conventions, informal campus relations, or other on-the-job relations. Work with graduate students and undergraduates to develop dissertations, seminar papers, and term papers.

Work with different people to provide a variety of interaction. Arrange to be asked questions by people with a variety of orientations, including sincere inquiry, skepticism, cynicism, and even a touch of malice. Try to operate in an interdisciplinary environment for a great variety of perspectives. Apply one's creative ideas to see what happens in practice.

B. Commitments as Pushing Factors

Accept a commitment to write an article, a book chapter, or a conference paper on how to deal with a policy problem. That is likely to generate new alternatives. Teach in those fields I which one wants to generate policy alternatives. Take on obligations to co-author articles, chapters, or papers.

Take on obligations to do consulting work which involves generating alternatives. Prepare grant proposals. Arrange for competitive situations as a stimulus to developing new ideas.

II. Facilitators

A. Literature

Consult the literature in the field. There may be lots of alternatives already suggested. There are some software checklists that might be worth trying such as "Trigger" published by Thoughtware and the "Idea Generator" published by Experience in Software, Inc., 2039 Shattuck Avenue, Suite 401, Berkeley, CA 94701. Keep up with the newest ideas in various policy fields. Read provocative literature. Know the general literature in the fields in which one is interested.

Read some of the literature on creativity including the list of references attached to this article. Have theoretical frameworks that can serve as checklists and prods for developing alternatives. Be familiar with the methods of knowing, including how to inductively generalize, how to deduce conclusions, how to determine what authorities hold, and how to do sensitivity analysis. Think about ways of generating ideas like this article, or adding to this article.

B. Working Style

Talk Out Loud About The Possible Alternatives. Dictating Is Better Than Thinking In Generating Ideas. Delegate Work To Others In Order To Have More Time To Think. Have A Pencil And Paper Handy At All Times Or Dictating Equipment To Write Or Dictate Ideas That Come To One's Mind Before They Are Lost. Schedule Time Periods For Creative Development And Implementing Of Ideas. The More Time Periods The Better. Occasionally Travel In Order To Provide A Variety Of Environments.

C. Multi-Criteria Decision-Making

Try listing some alternative, even if one only has in mind one or two alternatives to begin with. Merely trying to generate a list tends to result in more items being listed than one originally had in mind, or thought one had in mind. After generating some alternatives, then some criteria for evaluating them. That will lead to more alternatives. After generating alternatives and criteria, then generate some relations between the alternatives and criteria. That will lead to more alternatives. After generating alternatives, criteria, relations and initial conclusions, then do various forms of sensitivity analysis designed to determine what it would take to bring a second-place or other-place alternative up to first place. That may generate still more alternatives.

If there is a situation where there are two conflicting sides, each one favoring a different alternative, look to see what kind of alternative could maybe satisfy the goals of both sides. Also look to the possibility of a compromise alternative that will partially satisfy each side if it is not possible to find an alternative that will fully satisfy both sides. Then observing how the alternatives score on the criteria, ask how each alternative can be improved. Try to convert the alternatives, criteria, relations, tentative conclusions, and sensitivity analysis into a publishable table with notes. That may generate new alternatives.

III. PULLING FACTORS: REWARDS

Be motivated to want to generate alternatives. Arrange to be in situations where one is rewarded for generating alternatives, such as recognition, grants, publishing opportunities, graduate students, consulting opportunities, etc. Nonintellectual rewards can also be arranged for. That might include money, power, love, food, sleep, pure recreation, etc. Operate in a permissive environment that encourages experimentation and new ideas. The earlier one can get into such an environment the better, preferably starting at birth.

Some people use heredity as an excuse for not being creative. In both areas, there is a substantial range in which each person can operate. If one is more determined, then one can operate closer to the top (rather than the bottom) of one's inherited range. Creativity is probably less a matter of heredity than intelligence is. It is more susceptible to the kind of pushing, facilitating, and pulling factors mentioned above. Thus one can more easily arrange to be a more creative person than one can arrange to be a brighter person by seeking more favorable occurrences of those factors. Doing so can be rewarding in itself, as well as producing the kinds of rewards mentioned above. The broader rewards accrue not only to the individual, but also the many potential beneficiaries of individual creativity. It is an ability well worth stimulating by both society and by one's self.

IV. IMPROVING CREATIVITY BY MIRIAM MILLS

A. Juxtaposition

Try to juxtapose facts and observations. Come up with different views. Winston Churchill was aware of juxtaposition and when a British Admiral radioed him to say his task force was continuing to follow the Bismarck, but was running out of fuel and requested permission to return to base for refueling, Churchill said, "Continue to follow, we'll tow you home."

B. Multiple Answers

When we've come up with answers, we usually stop after the first solution is at hand. It's almost as if we believe the first answer provides the only way instead of one way. Charles DeBono, who has written extensively on creativity, says the search for alternative ways of looking for things is not natural. The natural tendency of the mind is to become impressed by the most probable interpretation and then to proceed from there.

C. Imagination

Not everybody seems to have the ability to form mental images. The exercise becomes easier. No man can exactly evaluate all the twists and turns and capacities of human genius, stupidity, or the incapacity of will.

D. Group Creativity

Now this is brainstorming. This has been described by William J. Gordon in *Cynectics*, New York Collier Books, 1968, which is fairly straightforward, including to: (1) identify and understand the problem, (2) collect relevant information, (3) mull it over, (4) speculate, (5) develop ideas, (6) select the best idea, and (7) implement it.

E. Creative Dreams

Sometimes real life is solved in dream sequence. To obtain creative answers, the following has been recommended: (1) clearly formulate the desired dream, (2) accept the fact that it is possible to induce dreams, (3) concentrate your attention patiently and persistently. This comes from Patricia Garfield, Creative Dreaming, New York, Simon Schuster, 1975.

F. The Opposite Approach

Reverse psychology has sometimes been used. Many negotiating examples where a person takes the opposite approach work out. An example is the wife who wants the husband to take out the garbage. He tells her he forgot. One day she said, "the garbage looks good near the door. Let's leave it there. It gives the kitchen an elegant atmosphere." The husband, amused, took the garbage out.

G. Concentration

Albert Einstein was supposed to be so good at concentration, he forgot where he was or had been. After meeting a student near the cafeteria, the student started to walk away. When Einstein asked, "which way was I walking when you stopped to talk to me?" The student asked what difference it made, and Einstein responded, "if I was walking towards the cafeteria, it meant I was on my way to lunch. On the other hand, if I was walking away from it, it means I've already eaten my lunch."

H. Association

Robert Frost, the noted American poet, said an idea is a feat of association. It is the function of creative people to perceive the relations between thoughts or things or forms of expression that make them utterly different and to combine them into some new forms--the power to connect the seemingly unconnected.

I. Visualization of the Problem

We should use our memory to determine situations that were similar to the one at hand or to use a fantasy or daydream to project where you want to be in the future. As you allow yourself to flash back and use your memory, write down the experiences and solutions and processes you went through and emotions you felt.

J. Restate the Problem in a Way That is Negative

Negative to what you want the ultimate outcome to be. In this way what you in essence do, is determine what you don't want, and use the negatives to form positives as to the ultimate outcome of a particular situation. You must write down again the things that please you and those that displease.

K. Listen to Ourselves on a Tape Recorder

One way to improve our negotiation skills is to listen to ourselves on a tape recorder prior to an important negotiation. You can merely practice your introductory remarks and statement of the problem. Another point would be to listen to how you sound and also have a friend take a role of the opposing negotiator. By reversing roles you have a chance to look at the problem through the eyes of your opponent.

NOTES

1. From S. Nagel and Miriam Mills, *Professional Developments in Policy Studies* (Greenwood Press, 1993), 115-120.
2. From Miriam K. Mills, *Negotiating in the Workplace* (Bell Labs, 1985).

Chapter 11

CREATIVE PROBLEM SOLVING

James Higgins
Rollins College

Not too many years ago, problem-solving was defined largely as a rational effort. As scientists and management researchers tried to improve the problem-solving process, they focused on analysis and quantitative factors. But in recent years we have come to realize that a strictly rational approach misses the whole point of problem-solving. Creativity is vital to successful problem solving. The problem-solving process therefore has come to be referred to as the creative problem-solving process or CPS.

There are eight basic stages in the creative problem solving process: (1) analyzing the environment, (2) recognizing a problem, (3) identifying the problem, (4) making assumptions, (5) generating alternatives, (6) choosing among alternatives, (7) implementing the chosen solution, and (8) control.

I. ANALYZING THE ENVIRONMENT

If you're not constantly searching for problems (which, as defined here, include opportunities), how will you know if they exist? And how can you solve problems or take advantage of opportunities if you don't know they exist? Most strategists believe that firms must be prepared to respond quickly to problems and opportunities in order to be successful in the future. Thus, being able to recognize problems and opportunities as soon as they occur, or even before they occur, is vital to success. Both internal and external organizational environments must be constantly and carefully monitored for signs of problems or opportunities. In this stage of the process, you are gathering information. Information gained during the control stage of CPS is vital to this stage of the process. Royal Dutch Shell Oil Company spends millions of dollars annually tracking its competition and the economy, and learning about its customers, for just one type of information systemCthe strategic information system. It also trains all levels of management to look for weak signals of environmental change. It spends thousands of man-hours creating forecasts/ scenarios of possible futures, all to enable it to solve strategic and operational problems better. The individual problem-solver must also spend time and money searching the environment looking for signals of problems or opportunities. For example, spend a few minutes to look at your internal and external organization environments. What is happening that might lead to problems or opportunities?

II. RECOGNIZING A PROBLEM

You need to be aware that a problem or opportunity exists before you can solve it or take advantage of it. It is from the information gathered in analyzing the environment that you will learn that a problem or opportunity exists. Often, however, the problem- solver has only a vague feeling that something is wrong or that an opportunity exists. A gestation period seems to occur in which information from the environment is processed subconsciously and the existence of a problem or opportunity eventually registers at the conscious level. For example, when Mikio Kitano, Toyota's production guru, began analyzing the firm's manufacturing cost information in the early 1990s, he intuitively sensed that something was wrong. The firm simply wasn't saving as much money as it should from all of the automation and robotization that it had just completed. He believed it was because robots were being used when human beings could do the job just as well, at less cost. Other top managers doubted him, but in the end he proved that he was right saving Toyota millions of dollars in unnecessary investment.

III. IDENTIFYING THE PROBLEM

The problem identification stage involves making sure the organization's efforts will be directed toward solving the real problem rather than merely eliminating symptoms. This stage also involves establishing the objectives of the problem-solving process and determining what will constitute evidence that the problem has been solved. The outcome of this stage is a set of decision criteria for evaluating various options.

Both rational and intuitive thinking may occur at this stage, but identification is largely a rational process. Key questions to be asked include the following:

1. What happened or will happen?
2. Who does it or will it affect?
3. Where did it or will it have an impact?
4. When did it or will it happen?
5. How did it or will it occur?
6. Why did it or will it occur?
7. What could we do to be more successful?

In asking these questions, you are primarily interested in getting to the core problem or identifying the real opportunity.

IV. MAKING ASSUMPTIONS

It is necessary to make assumptions about the condition of future factors in the problem situation. For example, what will the state of the economy be when the new product is to be launched? Or, how will your manager react to a suggestion? Remember that assumptions may be a major constraint on the potential success of a solution, or may cause you to over-estimate the potential of a particular alternative to solve the problem effectively. One of my assumptions was that there was a growing number of people interested in innovation processes. When I started in 1985, my assumption was wrong. But by 1993 it was right.

V. GENERATING ALTERNATIVES

Generating alternatives involves cataloging the known options (a rational act) and generating additional options (a rational and intuitive act). It is in this stage that most of the creativity processes are very helpful.

To the extent that you can clearly identify and formulate useful options, you can maximize the chances that a problem will be solved satisfactorily. The purpose of generating alternatives is to ensure that you reach the selection stage of CPS with enough potential solutions. Creative techniques for generating alternatives can help you develop many more possible solutions than you might come up with otherwise.

Generating alternatives is partly a rational and partly an intuitive exercise. It's rational in that you follow a series of steps. It's intuitive in that these steps are designed to unleash your intuitive powers so that you can use them effectively. In this stage, you should be more interested in the quantity of new ideas than in their quality. For most people, creativity reaches its highest levels in this stage of CPS. When Apple Computer Corporation's engineers designed the "Newton," the firm's new personal digital assistant computer (a small computer designed to help people in a wide range of jobs), they generated hundreds of alternative capabilities for the machine. In the end, several major ones were chosen over the others.

VI. CHOOSING AMONG ALTERNATIVES

Decision-making should be based on a systematic evaluation of the alternatives against the criteria established earlier. A key, very rational part of this process involves determining the possible outcomes of the various alternatives. (See Figure 2.2) This information is vital in making a decision. The better the job done in generating alternatives and determining their possible outcomes, the greater the chance that an effective choice will be made. The choice process is mostly rational, but very skilled decision-makers rely on intuition as well, especially for complex problems.

When Honda engineers pioneered the development of an engine that would get 55 miles per gallon, they had several alternatives to choose from. Important to their decision of the technology they chose, were the impacts of the new technology on the costs of production, compatibility with existing transmissions, and so on. Each possible technology had to be evaluated for its impact on these factors. Similarly, McDonalds Corporation, in considering new menu items for its fast food restaurants, has hundreds to choose from. Each potential menu item has to be evaluated against important criteria such as freezability (all McDonalds' ready-made foods are frozen), compatibility with other menu items, taste, customer demand, and cost/price relationships. They chose items like pizza because it fit these criteria. Conversely when Wayne Sanders, head of Kimberly-Clark's diaper division bet on Huggies Pull-Ups, he did so totally from intuition. The product looked promising but development proved difficult. He stayed with the product and eventually he was proven right. At the end of 1991, the product had 31% of the U.S. market.

VII. IMPLEMENTATION

Once you have a clear idea of what you want to do and a plan for accomplishing it, you can take action. Implementation requires persistent attention. This means accounting for details and anticipating and overcoming obstacles. Set specific goals and reasonable deadlines, and gain the support of others for your solution. Implementation is a series of problems and opportunities.

When General Mills Restaurants, a subsidiary of General Mills, Inc., began a total quality management program for its Olive Garden chain, it paved the way for adaptation at all sites by providing a lengthy training and development program. In addition, success stories were chronicled and distributed on video tape to all restaurants.

VIII. CONTROL

Evaluating results is the final, and often overlooked, stage in the creative problem-solving process. The purpose of the evaluation is to determine the extent to which the actions you took have solved the problem. This stage feeds directly into the environmental analysis stage, which begins a new cycle of creative problem-solving. It is important at this stage to be able to recognize deficiencies in your own solutions if necessary. If you can admit to making mistakes or changing your mind without feeling defensive or embarrassed, you have acquired the skill of open-minded adaptation. This often requires objective thinking, intellectual courage, and self-confidence. At Federal Express, group decisions based on CPS are part of the everyday routine, and so is control. For example when one team solved problems related to sorting packages, they were required to track results and make further improvements.

NOTES

1. This is an excerpt from the chapter on "The Creative Problem Solving Process" in James M. Higgins, *101 Creative Problem Solving Techniques: The Handbook of New Ideas for Business* (New Management Publishing Company, 1994). James Higgins is on the faculty of the Crummer Graduate School of Business at Rollins College in Winter Park, Florida. He is also the head of James M. Higgins and Associates Inc.

Chapter 12

DE BONO'S THINKING COURSE

Edward de Bono

What I have written in this book is based on many years of experience in the teaching of thinking in a practical manner to different ages, abilities and cultures. It is only too easy to sit down in a corner and to analyze what thinking ought to be and then to propose this analysis as a way of teaching thinking. That can do—and does—great damage to the practical teaching of thinking.

One aspect of the teaching of thinking is the need to remove certain misconceptions and to undo certain habits. For example, we really do need to stop considering thinking as simply intelligence in action. We do need to think of it as a skill that can be developed by everyone. We do need an awareness of the intelligence trap. We do need to encourage the self-image of "I am a thinker."

We also need to appreciate the domination of Western thinking habits by the negative idiom: clash, criticism and dialectics. We need to need to put negative thinking in its proper place as part of thinking. We need to put creative, constructive and design thinking before negative thinking.

We need to change our conceptions about thinking and action. To effect this change we need a concept such as "operacy" which gives status to the thinking involved in doing. We need to appreciate effectiveness and not just intellectual games.

We need to understand the major role of perception in thinking. We need to understand how perception works as a self-organizing patterning system with all that follows. For example, lateral thinking then follows directly and logically.

We need to place emotions, feelings and values in their proper perspective. In the end they are the most important part of thinking-- but only if they are used in the end rather than at the beginning.

We need to understand the practical value of being formal and deliberate about thinking instead of just waffling about. In the end we may prefer the habits, attitudes and strategies to become second nature but they will not become that just by our wishing it to be so. The formal and deliberate stages have to come first.

I have devoted a certain amount to these matters of understanding, appreciation, putting things in perspective, undoing misconceptions and attempting to trigger insights into thinking. At times the case may have been overstated and put too harshly, but my experience in the field has suggested the necessity for this. The biggest enemy of thinking is the feeling that our thinking is pretty good anyway and we do not need to do anything about it. I do not subscribe to this view. I think we have done well in technical matters and appallingly elsewhere. I believe we would have progressed much faster if we had been less complacent about our thinking skills and less inclined to delegate thinking to those who were using an antiquated idiom.

At times it has been necessary to create new words to focus better upon a concept. For example-- it was necessary to invent the term lateral thinking many years ago in order to focus upon an area which overlaps with creativity but is quite distinct. The word "po" is another such necessary invention, which arises directly from the logic of patterning systems. I have introduced other concepts such as movement value of an idea, exlectics as distinct from dialectics, logic-bubble to describe in a direct way the complex of perceptions and structure within which another person acts logically, operacy as distinct from description-type thinking. These are all offered as serious and necessary concepts. I believe they ought to be part of the language because without new words we cannot hold new concepts—they just drift off into the old concepts if we have to use the old words.

Then there are descriptive phrases like (1) intelligence trap, (2) Everest effect, (3) Village Venus effect, (4) shooting questions and fishing questions, (5) dense reading, and (6) decision preframe and postframe. These have only a descriptive or communication value. Those that are convenient may survive and those that are unnecessary will disappear. It is enough that they will have served to communicate an idea.

Finally we come to the specific tools on the attention-directing techniques. Those who wish to understand the full purpose behind these may want to read my book *Teaching Thinking*. I am well aware that a mass of initials such as PMI, CAF, C & S, AGO, OPV, HV and LV seem highly artificial and unnecessary. Indeed this is exactly what the teachers complained about when I first introduced the initials in the CoRT thinking lessons. This was before the lessons had been used. After some experience the teachers came back and asked for more such "shorthand devices." They had found that in practice there is a need for a strange, simple instruction that one can give to one's own thinking or the thinking of others. Whether we like it or not, the instruction "do a PMI" is more powerful than exhortation to look always at both sides of the matter. This is not surprising because that is how patterning systems work.

These tools (PMI, etc.) can be practiced deliberately and the practicer feels that he is making progress in mastering that particular tool. The operation then enters his repertoire of concepts as an "executive concept"—in other words he learns action concepts not just description concepts.

As the reader may well imagine, I have, over the years, lived through endless attacks about jargon and artificiality. These are made by people with no practical experience of teaching thinking and who find it easier to fasten onto this point than to discuss the basic concepts. In the end practicality must win. Experience with the teaching of thinking to thousands of adults and youngsters supports the use of these "attention handles." As a matter of fact, I myself, dislike jargon and that is why I avoid the usual psychological jargon since I am not writing for psychologists.

There are people who feel that if they pay close attention to their thinking then they will become self-conscious about it and become like the centipede that was immobilized by self-consciousness about which leg preceded which. This is a valid point and there are some elaborate schemes for thinking that do have this effect. Readers will have noticed, however, that the tools suggested in this book are no more than "attention-directing" tools. There is no elaborate and confusing scheme as to which steps follow which. You do your thinking as you have always done, but you may insert, at different times and in any order, such attention directors as PMI or OPV in order to make things more clear. If you were to forget everything except one technique (for example, the PMI) you would still have gained something. In an elaborate scheme if you forget part of it you are not only confused but also lost.

Must one really practice thinking in the deliberate manner suggested. The answer is yes. There are insights, understandings and awarenesses that will improve your thinking just as you read about them. For example, your attitude to negative thinking might change. But there are other aspects which do require *deliberate* practice. For instance, everyone has the general intention of considering other people. You can read any amount you like about cooking or golf or driving a car but in the end it is practice that matters.

Chapter 13

BOPPING OUT OF THE BOX

Michael F. Shaughnessy
Eastern New Mexico University
Raymond Considine
Considine and Associates

In most businesses and industries, workers and supervisors engage in the usual, mundane, routine, appropriately insipid and vapid thinking. In order to make money, serve customers and produce new innovative products, some out-of-box thinking is in order. All too often, it is quite difficult to get people to practice creative thinking, to engage in creative thinking and to integrate divergent thinking into their routine. This paper will push the envelope and try to force people to behave creatively and transcend their normal thinking. Creating a culture that thinks out of box is difficult, but it can be done. Innovative, fun ideas are imperative and experimentation has to be initiated. Here are a dozen really wacky quacky ideas that may help your employees to think above and beyond their normal capacity.

I. THE DANDY DOZEN

1. Obtuse, really divergent ideas can be offered both to warm up a group or to send new ideas in new directions.
2. The bathroom stalls should be seen as places where notes can be posted and posters conspicuously displayed. Shaughnessy (1993) has twenty-seven posters available from the American Creativity Association that were adapted from an article entitled "Daily Fostering of Creativity." These are available for review from the author or from the American Creativity Association.
3. Lunch hours should be punch hours wherein great ideas can be shared in a new venue.

4. Drives to work can result in ideas shared by cell phone. Car-pooling can result in dynamic ideas as well as save gas, oil, and the environment.
5. Perhaps once a month, staff should take Tuesday and Thursday off and work on Saturday and Sunday, or any variation on this theme. It may result in some new, different ideas as well as invigorated attitude.
6. Meetings should be totally reorganized to optimize creative problem-solving. Non meetings can be held when Ally McBeal is on television. Ideas may emanate from the music of the show or from the personality traits of the characters.
7. Instead of coffee, other beverages can be tried with different music in the background. Enjoy hot chocolate in the summer with Hawaiian music playing in the background. Korean music may stimulate different creative thoughts.
8. Attempt to de-educate people. All too often, we try to educate people to practice creativity. We need to get them to return to the fresh innocent childish thinking that we used when we were children in awe of the world.
9. Improve things, improve a product, improve a way of doing things, improve an approach, and improve your improvements.
10. Don't make it hard for them (your customers) to give you their money.
11. Use your senses and common sense. Make things smell nicer, fresher, and look brighter and be more melodious. Make things more tactile and handier and nicer to hold and more sensuous.
12. Make things simpler and sillier and larger and nicer-sounding, instead of smaller. One does not always need to be alliterative.

There are many other options and alternatives to enhance the climate of creativity. Some follow:

II. THE DEVILISH DOZEN

1. Have a Family Day at work whereby the kids come to see what Mom and Dad "do". The kids may offer suggestions and it is often interesting to see what comes out of the mouths of babes.
2. Meet in the park. It is often amazing how fast camaraderie develops "outside of the box" of ordinary business. Often the lack of air conditioning in colleges and universities, drives students and faculty alike out of the building. Often those classes are the most memorable and instructive.
3. Put up a dartboard in the conference room and use it whenever the team is deadlocked or hopelessly bored.
4. Who's that? Have everyone bring baby pictures of themselves. Have a contest to identify who is who. Throw in a few ringers to make it fun.
5. Hallway Hockey. Get some real hockey sticks and use wadded paper for a puck. Men and women can compete and the creatives or non-creatives can compete. Creativity can be determined by a method we don't have time to discuss.

6. Dress Up Day, instead of Casual Day. You may be surprised what different attitudes a formal level of dress can produce.

7. Take a different route to your office every other day. Purposely go a block out of your way where you've never been before. Refuse to be rushed. Be curious.

8. Write solutions to the city traffic problems. Take a lesson from Fulgham (what they teach you in kindergarten). Set your odometer and get off when it reaches 100 miles. See what's there. Pick out a company in the yellow pages and call them up and ask, "What do you do?" Ask them about their main improvements over the past year.

9. Be the host in the elevator or escalator. Sing or entertain. Get feedback from them as to what they think would improve their ride.

10. Do not pass Go. Refuse to let any small problem go by you. Solve minuscule problems. Untie phone cords. Re-arrange the office equipment you work with. Switch pictures. Make suggestions to merchants and building officers.

11. Be a kid. Keep asking "why?" Why don't kitchen sinks have foot pedals like doctors' offices do? Why aren't there gasoline caps on both sides of your car? Think about how much that would simplify life.

12. Be a December Santa Claus and collect money for charity and see how people react to you. See things from Santa's point of view or someone else's point of view.

13. People having fun are creative. Warning: nobody can be creative when they are angry. Have fun!

NOTES

1. M. F. Shaughnessy, "Daily Fostering of Creativity", *Focus* (American Creativity Association, 1993).

Chapter 14

SOURCES OF GOALS, POLICIES, AND RELATIONS

Stuart Nagel

Public policy evaluation can be defined as the determination of which various governmental policies or decisions is best for achieving a given set of goals in light of (1) the relations between the alternative policies and the goals and (2) various constraints and conditions.

This definition emphasizes four key elements in public policy evaluation:

1. a set of goals to be achieved within various normative constraints.
2. a set of alternative policies or combinations of policies that could be relevant to achieving the goals.
3. a set of relations between the policies and the goals.
4. the drawing of a conclusion from those goals, policies, and relations as to which policy or combination is best.

Where do these goals, policies, and relations come from? The answer includes four main possibilities:

1. authority; one or more persons, books, articles, or other reliable sources of information regarding the relevant goals, policies, or relations.
2. statistical or observational analysis; the analyzing of specific instances in order to generalize what the goals, policies, or relations might be.
3. deduction; the drawing of a conclusion from premises that have been established from authority, observation, and/or intuition.
4. sensitivity analysis; the guessing of the goals, policies, or relations and the determination of what effect, if any, the guessed values have on the final decision regarding which policy is best.

The four basic sources can be subclassified in various ways. For example, authority can be meaningfully discussed in terms of expert authority and general public opinion. Authority could also be contemporary or historical. Observation can be impressionistic or systematic, including statistical. Deductive approaches can be based on intuitively accepted premises or based on empirically validated premises. Sensitivity analysis is threshold analysis in which we want to know the break-even point, above which we should take one course of action, and below which we should take another.

I. AUTHORITY

Consulting authorities, rather than establishing the goals, feasible policies, or relations in a policy evaluation with original data or reasoning, can be a big time saver. Traditional social science tends to downplay introspective information-gathering methods, in contrast to non-obtrusive methods. In policy evaluation, however, perhaps more consultation with insiders is needed in order to obtain more meaningful information about relationships than can be obtained from the limited and questionable data records that are available.

Who constitutes an authority on goals, policies, or relations? The answer depends on the subject matter. The Supreme Court is an authority, for example, on what goals are legitimate in satisfying the right-to-counsel clause of the Sixth Amendment to the Constitution. The Court has said that saving money is not an appropriate goal, but that saving innocent persons from being convicted is. If, however, the issue is not where right to counsel should be provided but rather how it should be provided, then saving money is an appropriate goal. For this issue, the goals of a county board would be relevant because it generally appropriates money to pay court-appointed lawyers to represent the poor. Such goals might include satisfying local lawyers while minimizing expenditures. The board might, therefore, decide on a salaried public defender system, rather than on a less expensive but less politically feasible assigned counsel system or a less legally feasible volunteer system. For other policy problems, the key authorities might be legislative opinion, public opinion, the head of an administrative agency, or the like.

II. STATISTICAL OBSERVATION

Statistical analysis is the most systematic form of inducing generalizations from many instances or observations. It is generally used for establishing relations, rather than for establishing goals or feasible policies. Statistical analysis can, however, be useful in establishing goals or weights for the goals whenever the goals, rather than being ultimate, are instrumental for achieving higher objectives.

Accounting is a variation on statistical analysis. Like statistical analysis, it involves aggregating data, but accounting data is generally more precise than statistical analysis that is based on averages or the fitting of curves to scattered data points. A public opinion survey is not a variation on statistical analysis in the context of the typology of sources used in this chapter. Rather, it is a form of consulting authority in which the authority is the general public or a special segment of it. A statistical analysis (as a distinct source of information on goals, policies, or relations) involves a cross-tabulation, an analysis of the variation between averages, or a regression-equation analysis. These forms of statistical analysis involve determining a relation which is relevant (1) weighting goals, (2) deciding which policies are feasible to choose among, or (3) relating a policy to a goal.

III. DEDUCTION

Deduction involves arriving at a conclusion from premises that have been established by way of authority, empirical validation, prior deduction, or intuition. The more acceptable the premises are, the more acceptable the conclusions should be, assuming the conclusions have been validly deduced from the premises. Deduction is especially helpful where there is no authority and no empirical data for determining the information desired.

It is important to note that deductively analyzing premises may lead to an alternative policy that might be missed if one only relies on authority or statistical analysis. Authority is often not very creative in foreseeing problems, and statistical analysis is incapable of dealing with policies that have never been adopted.

IV. SENSITIVITY ANALYSIS

In policy evaluation, sensitivity analysis is a useful source of information about goals, policies, and relations when authority, statistics, and deduction do not provide clear answers regarding them. Sensitivity or threshold analysis enables one to determine how much room for error there is in weighting the goals, listing out the policies, or measuring the relations. Often, the controversy over precision in these matters is wasted because, within the range in which the controversy occurs, the overall conclusion as to which policy or combination is best is still the same. Sensitivity analysis also enables the policy evaluator to convert difficult questions about goals, policies, and relations into relatively easy questions, such as, "Is a given weight, policy, or relation above or below some threshold?" rather than, "What is the exact weight, policy score, or relation?"

In using sensitivity analysis to determine a set of feasible policies, we have to distinguish between a method that will provide a set of policies from which we can choose, rather than a method designed to arrive at an optimum policy. All four sources of information can be used to arrive at either feasible policies or an optimum policy.

V. INTUITION

Intuition is closely related to sensitivity analysis as a source of goals, policies, and relations. Sensitivity analysis frequently involves determining how different guessed values affect the optimizing conclusions. Intuition is also a form of guessing or basing estimates on strong feelings. Goals are sometimes accepted intuitively rather than being justified in terms of authority, statistics, or higher premises. This is especially so if the goals are general or near-ultimate goals, rather than instrumental. Policies may often be suggested as a result of a flash of insight, which is the case with hypotheses in traditional social science research. Although it is not generally respectable in social or policy science to arrive at relations through intuition, one can repeatedly guess at a relation until the reasonable possibilities have been exhausted and then see how these guesses affect the optimizing conclusions. One may find that it is unnecessary to be any more scientific than that, since all the reasonable guessed values may yield the same conclusion as to which policy is best.

Ultimately all goals and relations depend on intuition. Goals can be justified by appeal to authority, statistics, or deduction. However, how does one justify (1) the authority, (2) the dependent or goal variable in a statistical analysis, and (3) the basic premises in a deductive analysis? One can likewise ask for a justification of these justifications. In policy evaluation, one usually has an overall goal that is accepted intuitively, such as promoting the greatest happiness for the greatest number or satisfying the decision makers. Likewise, one can ask, why does policy X cause goal Y? The answer might be that there is a Z variable between X and Y which is caused or increased by X, and which in turn causes or increases Y. One can then ask, why does X cause Z and why does Z cause Y? At each stage of the causal regress, one tends to move further away from substantive policy and social science toward natural science and metaphysics. Ultimately, the question becomes, how do we know there is an X or a Y? That is, how do we know there is such a thing as a congressional statute or an American population that has social-indicator characteristics? In other words, on a philosophical level, we have to accept some empirical reality, such as the existence of the world. Fortunately for most policy evaluation, the goals in dispute are seldom ultimate goals, but rather instrumental goals that can be justified in terms of authority, statistics, or deduction. Similarly, the relations are seldom, if ever, metaphysical; rather, they can also be explained in a satisfactory, nonphilosophical way in terms of authority, statistics, and deduction.

VI. Some Conclusions

We can conclude from this analysis of the sources of goals, policies, and relations in policy evaluation that there are a variety of sources that can be systematically classified. We can also conclude that perhaps policy evaluation should be making more use of the variety of sources available. Unfortunately, certain disciplines tend to overlook some sources at the expense of others. Law and political science seem to rely heavily on authority as a source, especially legal authority. Psychology and sociology may rely too heavily on statistical analysis, which tends to overemphasize variables that are easily measurable and policies that need to be adopted before they can be evaluated. Economics and engineering often rely too heavily on deduction, especially mathematical modeling, which sometimes involves unrealistic or incomplete premises. By working with a combination of authority, statistics, and deduction, one provides a form of triangulation which increases the likelihood of arriving at more meaningful goals-weights, policies, and relations.

There is no need to argue over which source between authority, statistics, and deduction is the most desirable. Authority is clearly a big time-saver if an accessible and respected authority is involved. Deduction enables one to draw conclusions about goals, policies, and relations without having to gather original data, but instead by synthesizing already known information. Statistical analysis does constitute a more ultimate, but more difficult, form of proof. In any concrete policy evaluation situation, the best source depends on the subject matter and what is to be done with it. If the policy evaluation involves constitutional policy, an appeal to Supreme Court authority may be most relevant. If it involves the effects of a strike in the coal industry on another segment of the economy, a deductive input-output model may be the preferable type of analysis. If it concerns the trade-off problem of inflation and unemployment, a time-series statistical analysis may be especially appropriate in relating inflation and unemployment to suicide rates, to the percentage of the two-party vote that goes to the Incumbent party, or other social indicators.

We can also conclude that sensitivity of threshold analysis is a useful tool in policy evaluation because even with authority, statistics, and deduction, it may still not be possible to arrive at precision in weighting goals, measuring policies, or determining relations. Sensitivity analysis enables one to determine whether increased precision is needed. It is only needed if the range of unclearness on a goal-weight, a policy, or a relation happens to encompass a threshold value. Thus, if the range of unclearness on a goal-weight or a relation is between 20 and 30, but the threshold value of the goal-weight or the relation is 10, then one can forget about clarifying the unclearness if one is mainly concerned with determining which policy is best. If, however, the threshold value is 26, then one should seek additional information from authority, statistics, and/or deduction to determine whether the actual value is above or below 26.

The purpose of this article has been to discuss the sources of goals, policies, and relations in policy evaluation. The article represents a synthesis of reasonable common sense, at least as a matter of hindsight. That is what good policy evaluation should be, namely, codified common sense. For thousands of years, many human beings have been making effective and efficient decisions. What decision science and policy science should now try to do is to capture the essence of what these good decision- makers have done implicitly. Less naturally competent decision-makers can then improve their decision-making or policy-evaluating skills.

NOTES

1. From S. Nagel, *Public Policy: Goals, Means, and Methods* (St. Martin's Press, 1984), 14-32. The full chapter contains a detailed example for each of the 4 sources of authority, observation, deduction, and sensitivity analysis for each of the 3 elements of goals, policies, and relations. There are thus 12 case studies.

PART FOUR: MOTIVATION AND FACILITATORS

Chapter 15

CREATIVITY AND CHILD-REARING

Stuart Nagel

A controversial issue in the study of creativity is what kind of child-rearing leads to creative children and therefore creative adults? We say "therefore" on the assumption that creative children are not subsequently stifled by a repressive society. We should change the word "therefore" to "generally" because this is not always so. An example might be Communist China. Chinese child-rearing is reputed to stimulate creativity. We may be seeing such creativity since the advent of market socialism under Deng Xao-Ping (8% to 13% growth) and before the Medieval Feudalism which followed the Sung Dynasty (paper, gunpowder, written language, abacus, Confucianism, printing).

What is there about Chinese child-rearing or child-rearing in general that may lead to creativity? The answer may be obvious regarding the causal relations, but not so obvious regarding the normative prescriptions. On the causal level, one can say that children need a minimum of food, health care, and love in order to be creative. If they are too weak from lack of food or from disease, they are not likely to be creative. Shelter and clothing may also be important where the climate is cold, although seasonal changes and moving one's home may also be conducive to creativity.

If those minimum biological and psychological needs are satisfied, then variations in child-rearing may produce variations in creativity. The key factor may be the amount of challenges and independence which children are given from the day of birth until they cease to be children at puberty. Challenges to a two-year-old may mean placing their food in containers that they have to learn to open. Independence may mean allowing a child to explore a room that has electrical outlets. Those who are more concerned about safety than creativity may object that learning how to open containers might mean the child can get into the aspirin bottle. Likewise, independence in exploring might mean the child gets electrocuted.

There is, however, a win-win solution to the dilemma of safety versus creativity. The win-win solution may be to have childproof aspirin bottles and to have childproof inserts that fit into electric outlets. A cynic might worry that the two-year-old will break through the childproof devices. It would be worth it if the result is improved creativity on the part of the children, adults, and society.

It is not racist to say that there are some cultures that have brattier children than other cultures. Instead, it is a compliment if brattiness goes with creativity. El Al flights to Israel are reputed to have many bratty Jewish children in comparison to Lufthansa flights in Germany or Aeroflot flights in Russia.

A related example is flying any airline to Japan that first stops in Manila. Prior to Manila, there are Filipino children playing vigorously. Subsequent to Manila, the Japanese children are more likely to be studiously reading. This is a partial factor explaining Jewish Nobel prizes and lack of Japanese Nobel prizes. Japan, however, learns well, as indicated by their high per capita income. The Filipino children do not grow up to be Nobel prize winners unless they become American professors, as some do. That gives them access to laboratories and colleagues which they may lack in the Philippines. A disproportionate percentage of recent American Nobel prize winners were born in Asian countries where they were socialized, but they then benefited from American university facilities and international colleagues.

Although child-rearing is important, it may not be nearly so important as other things in the Spring 2000 C+ News article on "The Causes and Effects of Creativity." One might say that preschool socialization is the least important of the six factors mentioned there, but it is nevertheless important. The other five factors are (1) free speech and press, (2) education and training, (3) libraries and information, (4) laboratories, think tanks, and conferences, and (5) rewards like royalties and honors.

Chapter 16

IMAGINATION

Bill Bradley
Presidential Contender

The innovators in basketball came upon their ideas through trial and error, by playing the game. Hank Luisetti of Stanford was the first player to shoot with one hand; before that, all basketball shots except the layup and the hook were two-handed. Joe Fulks of the Philadelphia Warriors concluded that he could get the edge on his opponent if he jumped and shot the ball from the top of his leap, and the jump shot was born. In the 1950s, Bob Cousy began passing the ball behind his back. He was considered a hot dog by traditionalists, but like most innovators he persisted because he believed in his idea-- besides the crowds loved it. Gradually, coaches saw that the efficiency and deceptiveness of the move paid off in easier baskets for teammates. About that time, Elgin Baylor entered the pro ranks. Baylor's tremendous leaping ability allowed him to combine the jump shot and layup; he was the first player who seemed to hang in air, defying gravity. Julius Erving and Michael Jordan are his direct descendants. Even kids with no leaping ability (myself included--the joke on the Knicks was that my peak leap equaled the thickness of a Sunday New York Times) tried to imitate Elgin as he moved around the basket, altering his shot by changing the ball from hand to hand and using the rim on layups to block his defender's attempt to reach the ball.

Innovation took place mainly on offense until Bill Russell and K. C. Jones arrived on the scene in the mid-fifties. As teammates on consecutive national championship teams at the University of San Francisco, and then on the Celtics championship teams, they changed the meaning of defense in basketball. Before them, it was like counter-punching in boxing: The offense would make a move and the defense would respond to it. Russell and Jones forced the offense to react. "K. C. thought differently," Russell wrote in his book. *Second Wind*:

"He was always figuring ways he could make the opponent take the shot he wanted him to take when he wanted him to take it, from the place he wanted the man to shoot. Often during games, he would pretend to stumble into my man while letting the player he was guarding have a free drive to the basket with the ball, knowing that I could block the shot and take the ball away. Or, he'd let a man have an outside shot from just beyond the perimeter of his effectiveness and, instead of harassing the player, would take off down the court, figuring that I'd get the rebound and throw him a long pass for an easy basket."

Russell in particular was a master of invention. Having concluded that horizontal lines defined the game better than vertical ones (notwithstanding the fact that more and more players were jumping higher), he was always conscious of the angle at which he did anything on the court. If he had to block a shot from behind on a man streaking for a breakaway lay-up, he would take a step to the left so that he could come from behind at an angle that would allow his left arm to block the shot and his body to land to the shooter's right, thereby avoiding the collision that would have earned him a foul. If he was attempting to block a jump shot, he tried to do it during the first foot of the ball's arc, which meant that his body had to be close to the shooter's body in the air; and he used a vertical leap with outstretched arms because that created fewer fouls than a leap forward, which would have carried his body into the shooter. He also knew that while a blocked shot pleases the crowd, it is only half the story; the other half is giving your team control of the ball. So when he blocked a shot, his aim was to bat the ball not into the crowd or against the backboard but to a teammate so that the fast break could begin.

Russell also pointed out that over 60 percent of rebounds occur below the rim, which means that positioning is more important than leaping ability. Knowing where a particular player's shot usually bounces allows you to anticipate where to be. Boxing out far enough from the basket increases the area you can reach whenever the ball caroms off the rim. Starting under the basket and backing (or assing) your opponent out toward the foul line can surprise him and create a similar space to gather in a rebound. More than any other player then or since, Russell mastered the game's mental aspects, but other great rebounders--Paul Silas, Dave DeBusschere, Moses Malone, Dennis Rodman, Jayson Williams-- also understand the subtlety of the art.

The most dramatic sports innovation I can recall was introduced by the high jumper Dick Fosbury in 1968, when he turned on his back going over the bar instead of going over stomach clown, which was the conventional approach. "I was told over and over again that I would never be successful, that I was not going to be competitive and the technique was simply not going to work," he said to a reporter after winning the gold medal at the Mexico City Olympics. "All I could do was shrug and say, 'We'll just have to see.'" The artist, the scientist in the lab, the technologist with a hunch develop ideas that change the world forever. These sports innovators remind us anew that one person can make a difference-- and has, time and time again.

Some players demonstrate a creative imagination in maximizing their modest skills. One of my teammates once said to me half jokingly, "You know, Bill, you're the best player in the NBA--from your wrist to the tip of your fingers." He meant that I had good hands, hands that got to a lot of places quickly. Often you can block an opponent's shot by sticking your hand into the area where he brings the ball up from a dribble for the shot, a move called "stripping him." When the Knicks played a team with a big center, I would often drop off my man and double team the center when he got the ball. More than a few times, while I was still facing the man I was guarding, I would reach back with my swatting hand and knock the ball loose from the center's grip. At a minimum I clogged up the area so that the center had less room to make his move.

Having good hands on offense means that you can catch a pass, make a pass, catch and flick a pass at will. In shooting, good hands help to produce a quick release--the speed with which you move the ball from where you received it to shooting position. Beyond good hands, really great passers have a kind of sixth sense that is spatial and rooted in superb eye-hand coordination and unusual peripheral and depth vision. And really great shooters plant their feet so that they have balance when they receive the ball. Imagination flows into your game when you devise your own ways of combining quick hands, good eyes, and good feet.

NOTES

1. This is an excerpt from the chapter on "Imagination: Dreaming Up The Game" in Bill Bradley, *Values of the Game* (Artisan, 1998).

Chapter 17

INSPIRATIONAL AIDS AT THE MKM CENTER

Stuart Nagel

I. VISUAL AIDS

The Miriam K. Mills Center for Super-Optimizing Analysis and Developing Nations has three VCR's that play inspirational videotapes almost continuously. The main tape consists of four composite tapes. Each composite tape consists of the last five minutes of six important movies.

The movies are chosen to represent the six policy fields of (1) economic policy, e.g., "Grapes of Wrath," (2) technology policy, e.g., "Madame Curie," (3) social policy, e.g., "Gentlemen's Agreement," (4) political policy, e.g., "The Life and Times of Robert Kennedy," (5) international policy, e.g., "For Whom the Bells Toll," and (6) legal policy, e.g., "Zola," which is about the Dreyfuss case.

The movies are also chosen to represent the four developing regions of (1) Africa, e.g., "Mandela," (2) Asia, e.g., "Ghandi," (3) East Europe, e.g., "The Bielski Brigade" who were Russian-Jewish guerilla fighters in World War II, and (4) Latin America, e.g., "Viva Zapata!"

Other inspirational tapes include (1) "Great American Speeches," (2) "The Presidents," and (3) "A Tour of the MKM Center." Each composite tape recycles the six movie endings to run for a few hours and then rewind. Hitting "play" causes the recycling to begin again. The volume is turned off to decrease distraction, while increasing inspiration.

1. COMPOSITE VIDEO ONE	3. COMPSITE VIDEO THREE
(1) Grapes of Wrath	(1) Louis Pasteur
(2) FDR	(2) Gandhi
(3) Democratic Party	(3) Exodus
(4) Form Whom the Bell Tolls	(4) Abraham
(5) Bataan	(5) The Ten Commandments
(6) Long Walk Home	(6) Gentleman's Agreement
2. COMPOSITE VIDEO TWO	4. COMPOSITE VIDEO FOUR
(1) Madame Curie	(1) Bound for Glory
(2) Mandela	(2) Robert Kennedy
(3) Zola	(3) Harlan County
(4) Norma Rae	(4) Viva Zapata!
(5) Bielski	(5) Singing for the Union
(6) Chariots of Fire	(6) You Got to Move

As mentioned under "The New Maze Logo" in the Introductory Material, the movie "In the Name of the Rose" may be the number one inspirational movie from the perspective of creativity relevant to free speech, merit treatment, and due process. Those civil liberties, in turn, facilitate expanded creativity and civil liberties in an upward spiral like the spiral staircase in the movie. The connecting links are as follows:

1. The villain in the movie is a priest who puts poison on Aristotelian books that he does not like to kill those who would dare to read them. Sean Connery, as a detective-priest, exposes the villain and denounces his form of book burning. The villain actually tries to burn down the maze-like library, but Sean Connery risks his life to save some of the most important books by getting out of the burning maze just in time.
2. Sean Connery exposes the villain with the aid of a woman who is accused of being a witch and with the aid of a disabled hunchback who is accused of being possessed by the devil. He denounces the anti-merit bigotry. Both people are shown to be highly competent human beings, but they are both burned at the stake.
3. Sean Connery is accused by the villain of heresy, and Sean is tried by the inquisition. The leaders of the inquisition are depicted as totally corrupt and evil.
4. For good measure, the movie also endorses improving the quality of life for the poor. They are shown to be living horribly wretched lives, while the higher officials in the church and state live in luxury. The peasants, however, revolt in the closing scenes.

This widely acclaimed movie probably would have gotten Sean Connery and others associated with it on the Hollywood redlist in the McArthyism of the 1950s. The movie, however, was made later when there was more artistic freedom in Hollywood and academic freedom in writing novels and textbooks.

II. AUDIO AIDS

The MKM Center has multiple CD players and tape players. They play inspirational CDs and tapes almost continuously.

The main CD player rotates through 50 CDs consisting of (1) union songs like "Solidarity Forever," (2) civil rights songs like "We Shall Overcome," (3) patriotic songs like "Stars and Stripes Forever," (4) ethnic songs like "Tzena, Tzena, Tzena," and (5) non-political folk or country songs like "Look at them Beans."

The performers include Woody Guthrie, Peter Seeger, Bob Dylan, Joe Glazer, Johnny Cash, Paul Robeson, Huddie Leadbetter, and the Kingston Trio. Each complete tape consists of six inspirational songs from various sources, such as the Smithsonian Institution, the Bear Family, and Sing Out. A tape or CD player plays at the east and west ends of the MKM Center and both downstairs and upstairs.

In addition to the important videotapes and audio-tapes, people working at the MKM Center are also inspired by the many murals, bulletin boards, doo dads, screen savers, flags, friendly cats, nutritious food, filing cabinets, and weekly flowers.

That especially includes the intellectual interaction regarding the implementing of productive output. The output emphasizes (1) publishing books, journals, and newsletters, (2) doing world-wide workshops, and (3) consulting with people in government, academia, and journalism. The subject matters are super-optimizing or win-win policy analysis and developing nations in accordance with the title and mandate of the MKM Center.

1. COMPOSITE AUDIO ONE
(1) This Land is My Land
(2) Reuben James
(3) Some Days Are Diamonds
(4) Impossible Dream
(5) We Shall Overcome
(6) Joe Hill

3. COMPOSITE AUDIO THREE
(1) Farmer-Labor Train
(2) Goodnight Irene
(3) North to Alaska
(4) Ol' Man River
(5) Look at Them Beans
(6) Which Side Are You On

4. COMPOSITE AUDIO FOUR
(1) 16 Tons
(2) Happy Days Are Here Again
(3) Stars and Stripes Forever

2. COMPOSITE AUDIO TWO
(1) Banks of Marble
(2) Solidarity Forever
(3) Keep Your Eyes on the Prize
(4) Hold the Fort
(5) Oh Freedom

(4) Alexander's Ragtime Band
(5) When the Yanks Go Marching In
(6) Tzena, Tzena, Tzena
(7) Marine Corps Hymn

5. COMPOSITE AUDIO FIVE
(1) America
(2) Quiet is the Night
(3) At the Back of the Bus
(4) Commonwealth of Toil
(5) We Shall Not Be Moved
(6) Roll on Columbia

Chapter 18

MONEY AS A MOTIVATOR IN NETSCAPE DEVELOPMENT

Michael Lewis
New York Times

On Sunday, October 10, the *New York Times Magazine* did a biographical article on Jim Clark by Michael Lewis entitled "The Search Engine." Jim Clark is the key entrepreneur behind Netscape and other recent Internet developments. The article tends to be a chronology of events rather than attempt to develop some principles for explaining technological creativity or creativity in general. The key principle is that the profit motive can be a great stimulus. In the case of Jim Clark, merely making a profit was not enough. He was and is explicitly motivated toward making billion-dollar profits. The words of Michael Lewis follow.

On the face of it, Jim Clark seemed poorly designed to pursue the new thing. He grew up poor in Plaineview, Texas, where poor meant poor. He had been an indifferent student and a cutup. He was one of those great bad examples to youth, who proved that if you really want to be a success in life, you have to start by rebelling against your elders. Expelled from high school during his junior year in 1961, Clark enlisted in the navy. In 1978, he landed in the Stanford University Computer Science Department. Here he specialized mainly in self-pity. "One day I was sitting at home," Clark says, "and I remember having the conscious thought that I was 38 years old, and I had achieved nothing. I developed this maniacal passion for wanting to achieve something."

In something like an instant, Clark changed his life. He reinvented his relationship to the world around him, and in ways considered normal only in California. No one who had been in his life would be there 10 years later. His wife, his friends, and his colleagues would all be new. Suddenly, the best computer science people in Stanford were seeking him out. Clark put the m to work on his private project, a little computer chip he was designing called the geometry engine. The geometry engine made it possible to create a simulation of reality on the computer screen, using three-dimensional graphics processed in real time. It was Clark's first taste of the new new thing. In 1981 it became the basis for a new company, founded by Clark and his students, called Silicon Graphics. Silicon Graphics became a multibillion-dollar company and Clark became a multimillionaire.

And yet the man was still miserable. Clark found that he was as ill designed for life inside a big corporation as he was for life inside a big university. The big corporation soon had a serious American executive from Hewlett-Packard named Ed McCracken, who kicked Clark upstairs into the office of chairman. There Clark sank into another of his dangerous depressions. All thorough the late 1980's he sowed strife and discontent in his own enterprise, complaining to underlings that McCracken was an idiot, that he could not see the future, that Silicon Graphics was doomed unless it perpetually reinvented itself. The idea Clark became wedded to, in the early 1990's, was to turn an ordinary television set into a computer. The telecomputer, he called it. The point was to enable the viewer to interact with his black box. You would tell the telecomputer what you wanted and it would fetch it for you. You could shop through it. You could send instant messages through it and receive messages back. You could order up any movie you wanted.

At first Clark believed the telecomputer project might end well. He talked about creating new applications for the telecomputer. To do that he needed young software talent, and to that end he called a 22-year-old not long out of the University of Illinois and new to the Valley named Marc Andreessen. Clark had seen a piece of software that Andreessen had helped to write in college, called Mosaic. Mosaic enabled its user to travel around this thing called the Internet. Why anyone would wish to do so was at the time unclear.

About the first thing Andreessen said was that he did not want to make a business of Mosaic. Clark did not care; he just figured Andreessen would know a lot of software cowboys. For the next month or so, Clark would spew ideas, Andreessen would jot them up in a business plan. Almost all of these ideas assumed the telecomputer was the future. Then one day, as Andreessen and Clark sat at Clark's kitchen table, Clark announced that he had changed his mind. This was not unusual. Clark was always changing his mind. Now he said that his telecomptuer was ahead of its time. It was too expensive to build.

"We could always build a Mosaic killer," said Andreessen. "What do you mean?" said Clark. Andreessen said that the University of Illinois had his software but that he also felt sure they would bungle any subsequent attempt to commercialize it. He mentioned that 25 million people were now using the World Wide Web, and their numbers had been doubling every year for a long time. Clark recalls: "I thought, Jesus, those are big numbers. I have never been in a business with those kind of big numbers. Eventually you were talking about all the people on earth."

The Internet. "All of a sudden it was clear to me when I looked at the Internet that I was looking at the personal computer in 1985," Clark said. "It was this slow, clunky technology but people were using it. And it would get faster. I realized that this was the thing I had been groping for." He and Andreessen hired Andreessen's college buddies who had written the code for Mosaic, and Clark had yet another team of young engineers to lead into battle. He called the company Mosaic Communications, then changed the name to Netscape.

This time Jim Clark was right. He was off and running down the dark tunnel with no end. Within 18 months the world's biggest technology companies realized they'd been trumped. Bill Gates sent a memo to his employees saying that the Internet now posed the greatest threat to Microsoft's control of the computer industry. The 1,000 Microsoft employees dedicated to building a telecomputer were reassigned to compete with Jim Clark's start-up. Thousands of others at Oracle and Sun Microsystems and even Time Warner were similarly redirected.

Clark's new company did not become merely a success. It torpedoed investments of hundreds of millions by the world's biggest corporations and reputedly smartest minds, such as Silicon Graphics, Time Warner, Microsoft, Sun, Oracle, AT&T. Thousands of people had more or less wasted billions of dollars, and whether they knew it or not they had been following his lead. Then, just as they all ran as a herd in one direction, Clark took off in another. And within six months he made them all look like fools. It was one of the great unintentional head fakes in the history of technology.

Chapter 19

BRAINSTORMING

John Heyer, Mark Norby, And Joe Lauck

I. BY GROUPS

Brainstorming is a technique developed by Alex Osborn, an executive of a major New York advertising firm, and first described in his book, Your Creative Power (1948) It is designed to increase the flow of ideas in small group meetings. The most important principle underlying brainstorming is that the process of generating ideas is completely separated from the process of evaluating them. Brainstorming sessions take place in two phases--an idea generation phase and an idea evaluation phase. During the idea generation phase, all judging and criticism of the produced ideas is eliminated--or rather deferred--until the evaluation phase.

In most conferences, such as town meetings and informal planning sessions, the standard format is debate, that is, proposal and criticism. This format is not notably successful in producing new ideas. Typically in such sessions, each new idea is met with a welter of criticism. Brainstorming is quite different from most meeting situations.

A. Idea Generation

During the idea generation phase:

1. All criticism of ideas is withheld until the evaluation phase.
2. Wild or even silly ideas are welcomed.
3. Quantity of ideas is encouraged.
4. Participants are encouraged to combine or improve on ideas already suggested.
5. The group acts as a whole, not breaking up into several small groups.
6. One person acts as a secretary to record the list of ideas.

A brainstorming group needs a leader who will enforce the rules. The first and most important task of the leader is to be sure that criticism is withheld. There seems to be a strong tendency in many people to respond to an idea by saying, "Oh, that won't work because...." An idea which is proposed as a joke may not be useful in itself as a solution of the problem, and yet it may aid the solution by suggesting a new dimension of the problem or by opening a new line of inquiry.

In a typical brainstorming session, the members of the group are allowed to propose ideas whenever they please. The possibility exists in this situation that one or a few of the group members will dominate the session, with the result that others may be prevented from contributing all that they could. To eliminate this possibility,

Bouchard (1972) has modified the typical procedure by adding a sequencing rule in which the members of the group take turns in offering ideas. He reported that groups using the sequencing rule produced more ideas than groups that did not use it.

If the group begins to run out of ideas during the idea-generating phase, it sometimes helps to review the list of ideas already suggested. When the group's ideas have been exhausted, it is time to move to the evaluation phase.

B. Idea Evaluation

In the evaluation phase, each idea is reviewed critically to determine if it is in fact a practical solution. A list of the ideas that the group considers most practical is then submitted as the group's problem-solving recommendations.

Osborn feels that brainstorming is helpful in producing new ideas for two reasons. First, the reduction in criticism during the generation phase allows ideas to be born and developed that otherwise might never have been suggested, or might have been rejected before they had received sufficient positive consideration. Second, Osborn feels that brainstorming sessions promote a kind of social contagion in which one person's idea inspires a better idea in another--an idea that the second person wouldn't have thought of otherwise.

Studies reviewed by Stein (1975) indicate that groups using the brainstorming technique do produce more ideas than groups that generate and evaluate ideas simultaneously. Further, most of these studies also show that the brainstorming groups produce more high-quality ideas.

We should note that Osborn recommends brainstorming only for certain types of "simple and talkable" problems--problems like, "How can we prevent stealing from the library?" and, "How can we get more foreign visitors to come to the United States?" Indeed, research on group problem-solving suggests that groups do better than individuals on some kinds of problems but not on others. Individuals are as good or better than groups in solving arithmetic problems (Hudgins, 1960), and in solving problems where each individual has all the necessary information. Groups are superior to individuals in tasks where the pooling of skills and information is important. For example, groups are superior to individuals for remembering a complex story (Perlmutter, 1953), and for solving prejudice-provoking syllogisms (Barnlund, 1959).

Barnlund suggests that the group is more objective than the individual because prejudices are not completely shared among the members of the group.

An Exercise: Form a group and conduct a brainstorming session. Suggested topics are:

1. Ways to save time
2. Ways to keep the city clean
3. Uses for discarded Styrofoam cups

II. By Individuals

While the brainstorming technique was designed to be used with groups, it can be used by a single person in private idea-generating sessions. The principles to be applied are the same. Separate idea generation from evaluation. Start with the idea generation phase, writing down ideas as they occur, without criticism. You should welcome wild or silly ideas, and you should try to combine or improve ideas that were generated earlier. The hard part in this phase is to control your internal editor--the internal voice of criticism which may lead you to ignore an idea that seems too dumb or trivial.

Just as with group brainstorming, when you begin to run out of ideas, you can review the list as a source to stimulate further production. When the ideas really have stopped coming, it is time to move on to the evaluation phase. Here you review each idea to select those that seem best for solving the problem.

An Exercise: Conduct a brainstorming session by yourself. Suggested topics:

1. How to increase your own efficiency
2. How to make your favorite annoyance less annoying
3. How to persuade someone to give you a job

Individual brainstorming sessions can be very helpful when you are writing (see Flower, 1980). Suppose that you are planning a magazine article on architecture for a teenage audience. To brainstorm, first generate all of the ideas you can think of that a teenager might find interesting or important about architecture. As you do this, scratch down rapid notes in the form of scattered words and phrases that will remind you of the ideas. When idea generation is complete, evaluate the ideas--that is, decide which ideas you want to include in your article--and then organize them into an outline. At this point, you are well started in producing your article.

III. By Companies and Agencies

How do the companies come up with ideas? Chances are, they found inspiration through brainstorming. Here are five steps to help make the most of your next idea-generating discussion.

A. Prepare

Successful brainstorming requires careful preparation. Here's how to start:

1. Set your goals and objectives. Goals are what you want to accomplish during the session. Examples: Create a theme, find a marketing vehicle appropriate to a particular venue, or select a venue and program appropriate to a specific audience. Objectives are what the project being created is supposed to do. Examples: Build brand identity, sell a product, explain what a product is or attract a crowd.
2. Pull together all the information you can. What information does the company currently have that will inspire your creative direction? Consider using company brochures and communication, product briefs, interviews with internal and external clients, samples of other current campaigns, Web pages.
3. Carbo-load creativity on an ongoing basis. Look for creative inspiration everywhere: movies, TV, fairs and expositions, museums, magazines, galleries, plays, travel, restaurants, flea markets, direct mailers. Bring any pertinent examples to the session.

B. Select Participants

Good ideas can come from anyone. Invite a variety of people, and your results will soar. Consider bringing in a writer, designer, project manager, product specialist or video technician. You may even consider bringing in someone totally unexpected (the receptionist, the janitor, the account exec's teen-aged son) and someone who represents the target customer or product user.

How big should the group be! Four to six people is an effective, manageable group. Invite more than eight or nine participants, and things may spiral out of control. To prepare participants, send them a briefing package (including an assessment of your objectives, challenges and needs along with the items collected in Step 1) prior to the session. Spend the first 10 to 25 minutes of the brainstorming session reviewing the package as a group. Encourage everyone to ask questions and make sure everyone understands the materials and procedures.

C. Find the Right Environment

The brainstorming "event" calls for and environment that enhances and furthers the creative process. The ideal environment:

1. Takes participants out of the normal work environment and stimulates creativity. If you want out-of-the-box thinking, get people out of the box-shaped conference room.

2. Does not represent the corporate structure. In a brainstorming session, everyone is equal. People need an environment that frees them from "organizational chart: constraints. An idea does not automatically gain acceptance just because it came from the company president.

3. Provides privacy and separation from the rest of the office and is free of distractions. No cell phones, fares, pagers or beepers allowed.

D. Follow the "Rules" of Brainstorming

For the best results, participants need to optimize their abilities to relax, leave inhibitions behind and most important, listen!

It's a good idea to use a moderator to lead the session. The moderator can prepare and present the briefing materials as well as lead and maintain control of the session. The brainstorming moderator doesn't have to lead the way creatively, but he or she must lead participants in following these rules:

1. Do not interrupt other participants. Everyone deserves a chance to say their piece.
2. Never say anything negative. The point is not to shoot down ideas; it's to generate as many concepts as possible.
3. Write it down! Someone should take notes on the session, typically the person responsible for the project (and preferably not the moderator).

There are many possible brainstorming procedures. Consider these techniques:

1. Give every participant one minute to toss out ideas. The group is free to discuss ideas as they come up.
2. Have participants throw out ideas in no particular order. If the group likes an idea, go ahead and explore it immediately.
3. Give every participant one minute to toss out ideas. No one else is allowed to comment. When everyone has finished, go back and discuss ideas the group finds appealing.

E. Know When to Close

Knowing when to move on, wrap up or reschedule is essential. Has the rate of ideas slowed down? Has the group lost its energy level? If so, take a look at what you've done and assess:

1. Have you fulfilled your goals/objectives?
2. Do you know what you have to do to continue the project? What is the next step?
3. Are there ways to execute the project?

If you can't answer yes to those questions, then you probably need to schedule a second brainstorming session. If you can say yes, then it's time to turn your ideas into action. Remember, ideas alone do not make brainstorming successful. Appropriate team members must leave with an assignment or call to action.

The references to the brainstorming sections on groups and individuals are:

1. D.C. Barnlund, "A Comparative Study of Individual, Majority, and Group Judgment," *Journal of Abnormal and Social Psychology*, 58:55-60 (1959);
2. T.J. Bouchard, Jr., "A Comparison of Two Group Brainstorming Procedures," *Journal of Applied Psychology*, 56:418-421(1972);
3. L. Flower, *Problem Solving Strategies for Writing* (Harcourt, Brace, Jovanovich, 11980);
4. L. Flower and J.R. Hayes, "The Cognition of Discovery: Defining a Rhetorical Problem," *College Composition and Communication*, 2(31):21-32 (1980);
5. B.B. Hudgins, "Effects of Group Experience on Individual Problem Solving," *Journal of Educational Psychology*, 51:37-42 (1960);
6. A. Osborn, Your Creative Power, (Scribner, 1948);
7. H.V. Perlmutter, "Group Memory of Meaningful Material," *Journal of Psychology*, 35:361-370 (1953); and
8. M.I. Stein, *Stimulating Creativity, Volume 2*, (Academic Press, 1975).

NOTES

1. John Heyer is the author of the brainstorming section on groups and individuals. His affiliation is not presently known. Mark Norby is executive vice president of the firm called Live Marketing. Joe Lauck is artistic director. They are the co-authors of the section on companies and agencies.

Chapter 20

WHY DO FEDERAL WORKERS INNOVATE ANYWAY?

John D. Donahue
Harvard Kennedy School

Innovation does happen in Washington. New missions are taken up; old missions are pursued in novel ways; standard approaches are refined to the point of real reinvention. The stories summarized in this volume offer only a small, unsystematic sample of the adaptation that goes on within federal agencies and thus cannot support conclusive generalizations about the sources of innovation. But they do suggest a few of the forces that cause agencies to do things differently, a set of catalysts that might be summarized (straining only a little in the name of alliteration) as pressure, promises, and pride.

I. PRESSURE

No matter how intimidating the impediments arrayed against it, innovation becomes more probable once the status quo is rendered unbearable. World War II required a wrenching transformation of the federal government, made up of hundreds or thousands of separate innovations (including the successful campaign to harness then-mysterious atomic forces to the war effort) that became possible only because the alternative to entering and winning the war was indisputably hideous. Few examples are quite so dramatic. But pressure--the prospect of dire consequences as the price of rigidity--quite frequently inspires change.

Sometimes the pressure comes in the bluntest possible form, as a mortal threat to an institution's existence. If the death penalty for failing to deliver value is seldom as clear and present a danger for public organizations as it is for their private-sector counterparts, it is by no means unknown. The Bureau of Reclamation's traditional mission had become patently unsustainable by the early 1990s. Its founding raison d'etre -- building dams -- had been eroded not only by a shift in public priorities, but also, ironically, by its very success in completing most of the more valuable potential projects within its domain. The bureau's traditional constituencies, feeling betrayed by the diminished pace of dam building, withdrew their support. Its traditional adversaries, in turn, were disinclined to waste many tears over the abolition of a lightly altered bureau. Thus deep reinvention became the only alternative to more traumatic change imposed from outside the agency. As this perception spread, it gave resonance to internal calls for change.

Similarly, the budgetary fallout from the end of the cold war tightened the resource constraints facing the Defense Personnel Support Center's customers in mess halls and quartermaster's offices throughout the armed services. As dwindling appropriations left supply officers progressively less slack, they became eager to ease their own budget pressures by seeking better deals on blankets, bug spray, bayonet scabbards, and the countless other items the center had traditionally delivered. When the center lost its monopoly on military supply in 1994, its future was suddenly put in Jeopardy, triggering a campaign of root-and-branch restructuring. Similarly, the Consumer Product Safety Commission, after years of wasting away as an organizational invalid, had to make a case for its existence if it hoped to endure.

External pressures need not be quite so stark. Even as budgets and head-count ceilings have tightened in successive deficit-reduction campaigns, very few federal institutions have actually been abolished. If nothing but the prospect of organizational oblivion could concentrate the minds of potential innovators, the Payoff would be meager. Dysfunctional or redundant bureaus can linger for decades as the institutional undead-drained of vitality, but still issuing paychecks. More commonly the pressure that inspires innovation comes in the form of new or intensified challenges, or a concatenation of separate stresses that together trigger change. The much-publicized prospect of a financial catastrophe echoing the savings-and-loan meltdown forced congress and the administration to deal with problems at the Pension Benefit Guaranty Corporation and made possible a series of innovations that might otherwise have been blocked. Congress's flat refusal to allow the Internal Revenue Service to simply update and expand its established procedures, as aging computers and growing demands rendered retooling imperative, created an internal seller's market for new ideas that sped the transit of over-the-phone tax filing from the drawing board to implementation.

By the early 1990s tightening budgets, expanding missions, and endless choruses of reproach from management and labor-similar in intensity, pulling in almost exactly opposite directions-made business as usual an excruciating prospect for the Occupational Safety and Health Administration. Elsewhere in the Labor Department, the Wage and Hour Division of the Employment Standards Administration found its traditional inspection model an increasingly futile method for holding accountable a complex, institutionally fluid, and highly competitive garment industry. And the sudden imposition of a new imperative-- limiting environmental damage-- inspired the Air Force's Aerospace Guidance and Metrology Center to rethink its technological fundamentals. While it differs in degree and character, external pressure helped lay the foundation for change in every case profiled here-and in most of the less heralded innovations throughout the federal government.

II. PROMISES

On the day John F. Kennedy challenged the United States to send a man to the moon, neither the technology nor the institutions existed to make the mission happen. But the audacious dream galvanized action, and in less than a decade the goal was accomplished. High-profile promises can alter the calculus of possibility and catapult missions to the front of the queue. Particularly when the promise serves to augment the resources devoted to an enterprise, it can powerfully catalyze innovation. Yet even if budgeted resources stay the same, the priority that comes with visible commitments can make it easier to sacrifice other institutional goals in the name of the explicitly anointed priority.

Several of the innovations profiled here owe much of their momentum, and sometimes their origins, to the national performance review (NPR), which was unveiled with great fanfare at the start of the first Clinton administration. Clinton and (even more directly) Vice President Al Gore wagered their reputations on the promise to deliver "government that works better and costs less." Federal appointees, from the cabinet level down, had personal and political stakes in delivering on the promise, given Gore's prominence in the administration and his obvious positioning for a presidential race himself.

The NPR featured a certain amount of hoopla and hucksterism, no doubt, but few who passed through Washington after 1993 would deny that it provided a thematic focus and institutional anchors that made it easier to market potential innovations internally. The visible commitment of top officials sent powerful signals throughout the bureaucracy-- reassuring the enthusiasts and warning the recalcitrant-- that the campaign would not fade away once a few speeches had been made. Explicit reinvention promises made by senior Labor Department officials (including Secretary Robert Reich and Joe Dear, the political appointee responsible for occupational health and safety) empowered people like Bill Freeman, the front-line architect of the "Maine 200" experiment with a workplace safety policy based on results. Many career officials at the Department of Housing and Urban Development (HUD) had long been frustrated by the clutter of separate programs that made their dealings with states and localities so awkward and process-ridden. But not until Assistant Secretary Andrew Cuomo decided to make his mark through administrative consolidation could the impediments be overcome.

Leadership matters, in short. But these cases suggest that a particular type of leadership spurs innovation. It is not so much a matter of pep talks and uplifting slogans, but of senior officials who put their reputations on the line with concrete public promises. Only by burning their bridges can leaders credibly commit that they will not retreat to business as usual when the status quo bites back. Leaders' promises, moreover, must be anchored in the organization's underlying mission and consistent with career staffers' seasoned assessments of what that mission means in practice. With the possible exception of HUD's Consolidated Planning, none of these reforms can be characterized as top-down. Most were fueled by an interdependent blend of front-office and front-line initiative, and several-including the innovations at the Immigration and Naturalization Service, the Federal Emergency Management Administration, the Internal Revenue

Service, the Labor Department's Wage and Hour Division, and the Forest Service-clearly started with career bureaucrats.

III. PROFESSONAL PRIDE

Pressure and promises can help to overcome the federal government's special impediments to innovation, but they are not enough. Necessity may be the mother of invention, but the record attests that this mother's fecundity is remarkably uneven. There are always pressures to deliver more with less, since federal resources fall short of claims even in the flushest of times. But these pressures only sometimes lead to true innovation. Similarly, a great many promises-even high-profile presidential promises-go unfulfilled. Challenges from the head office can improve the climate for innovation, but they cannot on their own force growth from barren fields, Other factors must aid in incubating innovation, and the cases here suggest the importance of intrinsic commitment and professional pride on the part of front-line federal workers.

Not one of the innovations celebrated in this volume would have been possible without the purposeful engagement of bureaucrats in the trenches. Personal commitment to an agency's goals among its workers can do much to counter the federal government's special impediments to innovation. Such motives are not unique to public workers, to be sure. But intrinsic commitment to the organization's mission is more indispensable in the public than in the private sector. A for-profit business could still operate, albeit badly, if its workers were motivated by nothing more than eagerness for income and the fear of its loss. But the federal government would promptly collapse. The innovations described here, like the many that remain unheralded, may have been nurtured by political pressure and committed leaders, but their parentage is usually found among front-line workers who were determined to make a difference.

Failure, futility, and irrelevance are soul-destroying for anyone with the slightest self-regard. Few federal workers can live comfortably with the thought that their work is pointless. When an agency falls to deliver on its mandate, or when that mandate drifts out of alignment with the public's desires, some bureaucrats salvage their dignity through self-deception; others seek more satisfying work elsewhere. But for many federal workers, pride forces reflection about how to do things better. By no means all such reflection is fruitful. Some potential innovators are earnest but inept; others lack a wide enough perspective to make reasonableabout what can and should be done; a great many assume, often correctly, that their superiors are not interested in new ideas and solace themselves with daydreams of what they could accomplish were it not for the chowderheads in the front office. But on any given day at any given agency, there are likely to be any number of latent innovations in the works.

Bureaucrats at the Internal Revenue Service's Research Division had long sought ways to simplify tax filing, and they dreamed up on their own the idea of filing by phone (along with other ideas for simplification that foundered short of implementation). External pressures for change helped them overcome the lawyers' objection that a tax return required a signature and a signature required paper. Why couldn't a "signature" be a personal code, the improvisers asked, This time the stars were in the right alignment-congressional politics, administration slogans, and budget cycles were all favorable-and the internal promoters of procedural simplicity won the day.

The intense eighteen-month reform campaign that reworked the Bureau of Reclamation's mandate while trimming the agency's personnel by one-fifth was, for the most part, the aggregate result of innumerable improvements suggested by front-line workers that leaders picked up once they started listening. The dismay of Forest Service workers at the declining health of the Carson National Forest played at least as great a role as the grief they were getting from environmentalists, loggers, and local residents in inspiring a new way to balance claims on the land.

The Immigration and Naturalization Service's policy of helping employers find legal workers sprang directly from the wounded pride of street-level agents. "There was a sense of frustration that we were really not doing the job, recalled one of the initiative's pioneers. "We would arrest the aliens and they would come back the next day, but everybody still got their paycheck. So we decided we were going to do something different." That "something different "--getting the jobs previously held by aliens filled by U.S. citizens, thus reducing the temptation for the employer to return to illegal labor--became national policy.

Bureaucrats at the Pension Benefit Guaranty Corporation (PBGC) were chagrined at being outmaneuvered by their corporate counterparts (to the detriment of retirees and of taxpayers); this eventually led to tougher PBGC policies and to new legislation that gave the rules teeth. A small group of career civil servants at the Labor Department, frustrated that the old strategy of raids and inspections was not curbing the growth of sweatshops, dusted off an obscure legal detail to amplify their leverage over companies that sold goods made in violation of the law.

Often the new ideas front-line workers develop require higher budgets. This is perfectly normal; it is always easier to think of ways to do more with more. Any healthy organization, whether in the public or private sector, chafes at resource constraints and can instantly, summon a dozen plausible uses for a budget increase. Since cutbacks require more managerial effort than do expansions-especially in the federal government-innovation is almost always easier if new missions are accomplished with new resources, rather than with budget and personnel "Trenched away from older missions. In recent years, as budget pressures reinforced the reigning imperative to do more with less, some workers dismissed the new dogma as self-evident nonsense. Others however, like the compliance officers at the Consumer Product Safety Commission, chose to emphasize economy and in so doing found a particularly hospitable climate for their ideas.

The power of professional pride as a spur to bureaucratic innovation is mostly good news for sympathetic observers of government reform. (It is not news at all, to be sure, for those who have worked much with federal bureaucrats.) Yet the good news is alloyed with some cause for anxiety. One worry is that bureaucrats may anchor their self-regard so solidly in accustomed ways of pursuing their missions that they resist radical shifts in strategy. For example, Wage and Hour investigators had come to score their successes by the number of employers caught in the act of shortchanging workers and forced to make good on the wages they owed. The "no sweat" initiative put the emphasis not on catching scofflaws, but on creating new incentives within the garment industry to raise the rate of voluntary compliance. In the (admittedly unlikely) event this strategy succeeded completely, wage and hour enforcers would never nail an offending employer. Veteran investigators had a hard time stretching their sense of professional satisfaction to include deterring violations, not just catching violators, and this presented a significant challenge to expanding the initiative. Other innovations will surely experience similar complications.

More generally, the greater the weight we accord professional pride as a motive for good performance—including innovation—the greater Washington's vulnerability to degraded effectiveness from any threat to the quality and morale of its personnel. This raises the stakes of attracting bright, energetic Americans into federal service and retaining them long enough for experience to season their idealism. As a causal contempt for federal workers becomes the unremarkable norm, self-respecting young men and women can be expected to shun the civil service, with a growing risk of poisoning the well of federal innovation.

Chapter 21

CREATIVITY AND SEX

Stuart Nagel

Some of the relationships between the concept of creativity and sex are:

SEX AND LIFETIME GOALS. Creative males and females may be partly motivated by a desire to please the opposite sex, or to please the same sex sexually if that is their sexual orientation. This could be conscious or more likely unconscious.

SEX AND EXTENDED DEPRESSION. People who are depressed are not so creative. Having self-confidence is important to creativity. This includes positive thinking whereby one can develop solutions to different problems. People may sometimes be depressed or lack self-confidence because they consciously or subconsciously feel sexually unwanted. Thus being sexually rejected can be depressing. Stated differently, being sexually accepted by those one is seeking can be uplifting and can help stimulate creativity.

SEX AND SHORT-TERM TIREDNESS.Being tired has an adverse effect on creativity. Being tired is different from being depressed. Everybody gets tired if they have not had sleep for a long time and have in the meantime been doing things that are physically exerting, mentally exerting, or boring. Being tired may occur among depressed people no matter how much sleep they get. The link here with sex is that sex is short-term invigorating. This can be contrasted with situations 1 and 2 above which relate more to long-term or intermediate-term. A person may be working on a difficult problem and be falling asleep. He or she gets a telephone call or a visitor from someone who is very sexually stimulating. After the phone call or the visit, he or she then goes back to work and comes up with a creative solution.

RELATED TO OTHER MOTIVATIONS. Necessity may be the mother of invention, but necessity of what? Sociologists say we are driven by four sets of goals. They can include (1) adventure, (2) curiosity, (3) material satisfaction, and (4) responsiveness of others including sexual responsiveness. All four separately or together can motivate creativity.

PART FIVE: WIN-WIN CREATIVITY

Chapter 22

WIN-WIN CREATIVITY

Stuart Nagel

There are about 14 different ways of arriving at win-win super-optimum solutions, whereby conservatives, liberals, and major viewpoints can all come out ahead of their best initial expectations simultaneously. The list could be used as a checklist to prod one's mind into thinking of solutions to specific problems.

I. MORE RESOURCES TO SATISFY ALL SIDES

A. Expanding Resouces

An example might include well-placed subsidies and tax breaks that would increase national productivity and thus increase the gross national product and income. Doing so would enable the tax revenue to the government to increase even if the tax rate decreases. This would provide for a lowering of taxes, instead of trying to choose between the liberal and conservative ways of raising them. It would also provide for increasing both domestic and defense expenditures, instead of having to choose between the two.

B. Third Party Benefactor

Some situations involve a third-party benefactor that is usually a government agency. An example is government food stamps, which allow the poor to obtain food at low prices, while farmers receive high prices when they submit the food stamps they have for reimbursement. Another example is rent supplements, which allow the poor to pay low rents, but landlords receive even higher rents than they would otherwise expect.

II. MORE EFFICIENCY IN ACHIEVING GOALS

A. Setting Higher Goals

An example of setting higher goals than what was previously considered the best while still preserving realism might include the Hong Kong labor shortage with unemployment at only 1%. Hong Kong is faced with the seeming dilemma of having to choose between foregoing profits (by not being able to fill orders due to lack of labor) and opening the floodgates to mainland Chinese and Vietnamese (in order to obtain more labor). A super-optimum solution might involve adding to the labor force by way of the elderly, the disabled, and mothers of preschool children. It also would provide more and better jobs for those who are seasonally employed, part-time employed, full-time employed but looking for a second job, and full-time employed but not working up to their productive capacity.

B. Decreasing Causes of Conflict

An example of removing or decreasing the source of the conflict between liberals and conservatives, rather than trying to synthesize their separate proposals, would be concentrating on having a highly effective and acceptable birth control program to satisfy both proponents and opponents of abortion, since abortions would then seldom be needed. Another example would be concentrating on a highly effective murder-reduction program to satisfy both proponents and opponents of capital punishment. Such a murder-reduction program might emphasize gun control, drug medicalization, and reduction of violence socialization.

C. Redefining Problem

Quite often a highly emotional controversy between liberals and conservatives may be capable of being resolved beyond the best expectations of each side through the approach of redefining the problem. They may be arguing over how to deal with a problem that is really relatively unimportant in terms of achieving their goals, as contrasted to a more important problem on which they might be likely to get mutually satisfying agreement. This involves seeing beyond a relatively superficial argument to the higher level goals that are endorsed by both liberals and conservatives, although possibly not to the same relative degree.

D. Increasing Benefits and Decreasing Costs

There are situations where one side can receive big benefits but the other side incurs only small costs. An example is in litigation where the defendant gives products that it makes. The products may have high market value to the plaintiff, but low variable or incremental cost to the defendant, since the defendant has already manufactured the products or can quickly do so.

E. Early Socialization

The socialization matter could be discussed across every field of public policy. If one is going to have a super-optimum society, then it is important what kinds of attitudes children have with regard to discrimination, poverty, world peace, crime, education, consumer-merchant relations, labor-management relations, free speech, and fair procedure. One could even say that the key purpose, or a key purpose of public policy, is to provide for a socialization environment in which children have socially desired attitudes on every field of public policy. If that is done properly, then a good deal of the problems of what policies to adopt will take care of themselves because the need for public policy will be lessened. If children, for instance, are imbued with more of the idea of judging each other in terms of their individual characteristics rather than in terms of ethnic characteristics, then we have less need for public policies dealing with racism because there is likely to be a lot less racism.

F. Technological Fix

The second level of insight is to communicate a recognition that such super-optimum solutions are realistically possible and not just conceptually possible. A good example relates to the ozone problem and the use of fluorocarbons in hair sprays and other aerosol containers. As of about 1985, such devices represented a serious threat to depleting the ozone layer and thereby causing a substantial increase in skin cancer throughout the world. The solution was not to rely on an unregulated marketplace, which normally provides almost no incentives to manufacturers to reduce their pollution. The solution was not regulation or prohibition, which tends to be evaded, is expensive to enforce, and is enforced with little enthusiasm given disruptions that might occur to the economy. The most exciting aspect of the solution (although the problem is not completely solved) was the development of new forms of spray propellant that are less expensive for manufacturers to use and simultaneously not harmful to the ozone layer.

This kind of solution tends to be self-adopting since manufacturing firms, farmers, and others who might otherwise be polluting the environment now have an important economic incentive to adopt the new low-polluting methods because they reduce the expenses of the business firm. This approach does require substantial research and substantial government subsidies for research and development as contrasted to paying the polluters not to pollute, which is even more expensive and often not so effective, because they may take the money and pollute anyhow. The business firms generally do not have capital for that kind of research and development, or the foresight or forbearance which public policy and governmental decision-making may be more capable of exercising. This includes international governmental decision makers, as well as those in developing nations.

G. Contracting Out

As for how the super-optimum solution operates, it involves government ownership, but all the factories and farms are rented to private entrepreneurs to develop productive and profitable manufacturing and farming. Each lease is renewable every year, or longer if necessary to get productive tenants. A renewal can be refused if the factory or farm is not being productively developed, or if the entrepreneur is not showing adequate sensitivity to workers, the environment, and consumers.

As for some of the advantages of such an SOS system, it is easier not to renew a lease than it is to issue injunctions, fines, jail sentences, or other negative sanctions. It is also much less expensive than subsidies. The money received for rent can be an important source of tax revenue for the government to provide productive subsidies elsewhere in the economy. Those subsidies can be used especially for encouraging technological innovation-diffusion, the upgrading of skills, and stimulating competition for market share, which can be so much more beneficial to society than either socialistic or capitalistic monopolies. The government can more easily demand sensitivity to workers, the environment, and consumers from its renters of factories and farms than it can from itself. There is a conflict of interest in regulating oneself.

H. International Economic Communities

An exciting new development with regard to international interaction to deal with shared policy problems is the international economic community (IEC). It involves a group of countries agreeing to remove tariff barriers to the buying and selling of goods among the countries as a minimum agreement to constitute an EC. The agreement may also provide for removal of immigration barriers to the free flow of labor, and a removal of whatever barriers might exist to the free flow of communication and ideas. The European Economic Community is a good example, but other examples are developing in North America, Africa, Asia, and East Europe.

The alternative of having an economic community does well on the conservative goal of preserving national identity, since no sovereignty is lost in an IEC, as contrasted to the sovereignty that is lost in a world government or a regional government. The IEC may also add to the national stature of the component parts by giving them the increased strength that comes from being part of an important group. Thus, France may have more national stature as a leader in the European Economic Community than it has alone.

Likewise, the alternative of having an economic community does well on the liberal goal of promoting quality of life in terms of jobs and consumer goods. Jobs are facilitated by the increased exporting that the IEC countries are able to do. Jobs may also be facilitated by free movement to countries in the EC that have a need for additional labor. Consumer goods are facilitated by the increased importing that the EC countries are able to do without expensive tariffs.

III. MORE COMBINATIONS OF ALTERNATIVES

A. Big Benefits on One Side, Small Costs on the Other

An example of this kind of SOS is the case of growers versus farmworkers in Illinois. The essence of the solution is that the growers agree to deposit $100,000 to begin an employee credit union. Depositing $100,000 costs nothing to the growers since it is insured by the federal government and can be withdrawn after an agreed-upon time period, possibly even with interest. The $100,000, however, serves as the basis for the beginning of an economic development fund that enables the workers through real estate leveraging to obtain a mortgage for building over $500,000 worth of housing as a big improvement over their current housing. The existence of the credit union also enables them to avoid having to get advances from the growers, which generates a lot of friction as a result of alleged favoritism in giving and collecting the advances. There are other elements involved, too, such as new grievance procedures and reports regarding compliance with other rules governing the working conditions of migratory labor. The essence of the solution, though, is that both sides come out ahead of their original best expectations.

B. Combining Alternatives

An example of combining alternatives that are not mutually exclusive is combining government-salaried legal-aid attorneys with volunteer attorneys. Doing so could give the best of both public-sector and private-sector approaches to legal services for the poor. Another example is combining tax-supported higher education plus democratic admission standards with contributions from alumni and tuition plus merit standards. Doing so results in universities that are better than pure government ownership or pure private enterprise.

C. Developing Multi-Faceted Packages

One can develop a package of alternatives that would satisfy both liberal and conservative goals. An example is pretrial release where liberals want more arrested defendants released prior to trial, and conservatives want a higher rate of appearances in court without having committed a crime while released. The package that increases the achievement of both goals includes better screening, reporting in, notification, and prosecution of no-shows, as well as reduction of delay between arrest and trial.

D. Sequential SOS

We can put the land reform example in with sequential SOS. The current verbalization does not say anything about encouraging the landless peasants to subsequently upgrade their skills to be able to take on nonagricultural work, or to upgrade the skills of their children. We could change the SOS definition to say simultaneously or sequentially. One drawback is that there is subjectivity and favoritism as to which alternative goes first. Simultaneity has an air of equality and equity; doing it sequentially may be essential in terms of developing feasibility. It is not so feasible to do various alternatives or goals simultaneously.

NOTES

1. For further details on different ways of arriving at win-win solutions, see "Ways of Arriving at Super-Optimum Solutions" in S. Nagel, *The Policy Process and Super-Optimum Solutions* (Nova Science Publishers, 1994), 15-70, and the book entitled *Creativity in Public Policy: Generating Super-Optimum Solutions* (Ashgate Publishers, 1999).

Chapter 23

WIN-WIN ASPECTS OF CREATIVITY

Stuart Nagel

Win-win analysis involves finding solutions to diverse problems, especially policy problems whereby all major sides can come out ahead of their best initial expectations. In policy problems, this tends to mean that both conservatives and liberals come out ahead of their best expectations.

In discussing the win-win aspects of creativity, we are concerned with such issues as (1) how to encourage creativity without consumers being taken advantage of, (2) how to encourage creativity without overly subsidizing relevant business firms, (3) how to develop the right combination of hands-off and government stimulation to encourage creativity, (4) how to develop research findings that are both valid and simple, and (5) how to strive for generalizations and case studies, simultaneously.

I. THE PATENT SYSTEM AND ENCOURAGING INVENTIONS

Preserving the patent system (as it is currently operating) tends to stifle some creativity by providing for a 17-year monopoly renewable once, but frequently renewed repeatedly with slight variations. It also stifles creativity by being the basis for lawsuits designed to obtain injunctions against creative competition. See Table 23-1.

Abolishing patents can hurt some creativity on the part of people who develop new inventions in order to obtain a monopolistic patent, although as of 1999 those new inventions may be for relatively small matters, rather than for new forms of transportation, communication, energy, or health care.

Changing the system by shortening the patent monopoly, requiring licensing, or having the government as an insurer against product liability can be helpful, but not as much as well-placed subsidies to encourage needed inventions. Well-placed subsidies could mean calling a conference of leading scientists and engineers to develop a list of

50-100 important needed inventions. The government could then announce the availability of grants and other monetary rewards to encourage the development of those inventions. The rewards could be worth more than a monopolistic patent, while still encouraging competition (rather than stifling it).

Table 23-1. The Patent System and Encouraging Inventions

Criteria Alternatives	C Taxes and Profits	L Competition
C Preserve Patents	+	—
L Abolish Patents	—	+
N Change System	0	0
SOS 1. Well-Placed Subsidies to Encourage Technology 2. Licensing on Royalties 3. Government as Insurer	++	++

II. ALTERNATIVES FOR PRODUCT LIABILITY

Common law defenses enable manufacturers to escape liability by arguing (1) they did not sell directly to the consumer, (2) contributor negligence by the consumer, (3) third party partially responsible, and (4) implicit waiver of the right to sue.

Strict liability means the manufacturer is liable for damages to the consumer if the product injured the consumer, regardless of the above common law defenses.

Comparative negligence means the consumer collects even if the consumer is partly negligent, as long as the part is less than 50%.

The SOS alternative as mentioned here provides for strict liability only after three years of marketing in order to stimulate product innovation and provide a time period for debugging product defects. A better SOS alternative might be to have the government be an insurer for the first three years so as to provide better compensation to injured persons while freeing product innovators from liability if they exercise reasonable care. See Table 23-2.

Table 23-2. Product Liability

Goals Alternatives	C Stimulate Innovation of Products	L Safety and Compensation
C Common Law Defenses	+	—
L Strict Liability	—	+
N Common Law Defenses with Exceptions or Comparative Negligence	0	0
SOS or Win-Win Strict Liability after 3 Years of Marketing	++	++

III. STIMULATING SOCIALLY USEFUL RESEARCH

The SOS emphasizes socializing people at an early age to want to discover new and useful knowledge. That means an emphasis on creativity and usefulness in elementary and secondary education.

Doing so is likely to result in more socially useful research than either pure market forces or making subsidies available, although such socialization can be combined with the stimulus of a free market and the facilitating value of a well-placed subsidy. See Table 23-3.

IV. VALIDITY AND SIMPLICITY IN POLICY ANALYSIS

Validity in policy analysis refers to internal consistency in drawing a prescriptive conclusion from goals, alternatives, and relations. It also refers to external consistency between the alleged goals, alternatives, and relations on the one hand and empirical reality on the other.

Simplicity in policy analysis refers to having as few goals, alternatives, and relations as are needed to capture the essence of the policy problem. Simplicity also includes an emphasis on simple arithmetic rather than calculus, operations research, or statistical analysis if possible.

Frequently policy analysts think of increasing validity by decreasing simplicity, or increasing simplicity by decreasing validity. The approach of using a decision matrix or an SOS table may provide greater validity by including goals that are normally difficult to work with using complex methods. Such goals may, however, be relatively easy to work with if simple methods are used that allow for a substantial margin of error. See Table 23-4.

Table 23-3. Socially Useful Research

Goals Alternatives	C 1. Freedom 2. Save Taxes	L 1. Usefulness
C 1. Laissez-Faire Encouraging What is Easy	+	—
L 1. Big Funding for Causal Research 2. Policy Research	—	+
N 1. Both	0	0
SOS or Win-Win 1. Socialization with Free Market 2. Subsidies	++	++

Table 23-4. Validity and Simplicity

Goals Alternatives	C Proper Form	L Democratic Understanding
C Validity	+	—
L Simplicity	—	+
N 2 and 2	0	0
SOS or Win-Win Striving for 100% on Both	++	++

V. GENERALIZATIONS VERSUS CASE STUDIES IN DEVELOPING KNOWLEDGE

Generalizations versus case studies is a controversial issue in the developing of new knowledge, but those two concepts do not lend themselves to conservative and liberal labels. Liberals tend to emphasize induction since it is normally associated with empirical observation. Conservatives tend to emphasize deduction since it is normally associated with reasoning from authoritative axioms.

The two key purposes of developing new knowledge are for better causal understanding and for broad practical knowledge. Those goals are also difficult to associate with the labels of conservative or liberal. Business conservatives emphasize practical knowledge. Intellectual liberals emphasize causal understanding. Within the same scholarly discipline, however, conservatives may advocate knowledge for knowledge sake. The liberals may then advocate knowledge that has implications for public policy or practical affairs.

Regardless whether the alternatives and goals are labeled conservative, liberal, position #1, or position #2, the SOS alternative might be a cyclical approach. Case studies lead to generalizations, but then generalizations are applied to specific situations which add to the case studies including the exceptions to the generalizations. Those new case studies reinforce or modify the generalizations, which then get applied to new case situations, and so on. The result is likely to better causal understanding than just relying on generalizations, and simultaneously better practical knowledge than just relying on case studies. See Table 23-5.

Table 23-5. Generalizations Versus Case Studies

Goals Alternatives	C Causal Understanding	L Broad Practical Knowledge
C Generalizations	+	—
L Case Studies	—	+
N Middle Range	0	0
SOS or Win-Win Cyclical Approach	++	++

Chapter 24

GOVERNMENT INNOVATION: WIN-WIN PERFORMANCE PAY

Stuart Nagel

Since at least the beginning of the Clinton-Gore administration, there has been a move toward developing new ideas for making government more effective, efficient, and equitable, especially more efficient. This movement is sometimes referred to as reinventing government. Much of the so-called innovation, however, may be new water in old bath tubs without the benefit of Archimedes creativity.

Nevertheless, some of the newness in public administration is both innovative and useful. Some of it is useful or valuable in both a conservative and liberal sense. That qualifies some of the reinventing as win-win.

To be more specific, there are at least two important developments in recent public administration that have win-win capabilities. One is performance payment. The other is win-win performance payment. The other is win-win vouchers and contracting out.

The purpose of this chapter is to give four examples of win-win performance payment with regard to economic, technology, social, and political policy.

I. ECONOMIC POLICY

The economic example relates to regulating the stock market. A key problem in securities regulation is the problem of stockbroker churning. That is the activity where stockbrokers encourage people to buy more stock than they should because the broker gets more commissions, or to buy not-so-desirable stock that pays a higher commission.

This analysis was stimulated by the news reports saying the Prudential brokerage firm had swindled its customers out of billions of dollars by lying to them regarding stocks that Prudential was selling. The Security and Exchange Commission negotiated a settlement to compensate customers who had suffered losses.

The conservative position is to be lenient. Doing so is conducive to the goals of minimizing regulation, leaving it up to the marketplace, and let the buyer beware. The liberal position is to be more severe, which is a reversal of positions from the reactions to street crimes. In the Prudential case, liberals wanted criminal prosecution or at least punitive damages.

The middling position was a settlement that provided for no punitive damages, but a waiving of the short statute of limitations, which would normally exclude many customers from being compensated.

The amount of money likely to be repaid is substantially less than the amount swindled. This implies a double standard toward big business swindlers. One could, however, argue that it is a double standard against relatively rich customers.

It normally is not desirable to have an SOS solution where criminal or near-criminal wrongdoing is involved. Doing so rewards the defendant and may defeat the deterrent value of punishment.

An SOS approach to business wrongdoing that is sometimes effective is to have government-stimulated competition. That could be done in this situation. The SEC could authorize ordinary commercial banks to buy and sell stock on behalf of their customers. Doing so would reduce the power of stock brokerage firms to abuse their customers. The threat of banks entering the brokerage industry might also cause more self-policing within the brokerage industry. See Table 24-1.

Table 24-1. Stock Brokerage Swindles

Goals / Alternatives	C Minimize regulation	L Deterrence of business wrongdoing
C Be lenient.	+	—
L Be severe.	—	+
N In between.	0	0
SOS or Win-Win Encourage competition by banks.	++	++

II. TECHNOLOGY POLICY

The technology example relates to regulating some of the bad effects of old and new technologies. A key problem in technology regulation is the problem of air, water, and other pollution.

The field of environmental policy involves both conservative and liberal approaches. Conservatives emphasize the role of consumers and the marketplace in restraining business from engaging in socially undesirable activities, like pollution. The liberals emphasize the role of the government in restraining pollution. Conservatives are especially interested in the goal of economic development, which may be interfered with by government restraints. Liberals are especially interested in the goal of a cleaner environment, which may not be achieved so effectively by relying on selective consumer buying.

A neutral compromise approach might involve giving business firms partial subsidies to adopt antipollution devices. Doing so would involve some requirements for receiving the subsidies, but less interference than regulation and fines. Doing so would help promote a cleaner environment, but there still might be evasions by business in view of the extra expense and trouble in complying.

A win-win policy alternative instead might emphasize subsidies to universities and research firms to develop new processes (that relate to manufacturing, transportation, energy, and agriculture) that are both less expensive and cleaner than the old processes. Those new processes then would be adopted by business firms because they are more profitable, not because the firms are being forced or subsidized to do so.

The new processes thus would achieve the conservative goals of profits and economic development, even better than retaining the present marketplace. Such a win-win policy also would promote the liberal goal of a cleaner environment, even better than a system of regulation, and without the expense of a continuing subsidy for adopting and renewing anti-pollution devices.

A specific example of such an environmental win-win policy has been finding a substitute for aerosol propellants and air-conditioning freon that is more profitable to manufacturers and simultaneously less harmful to the ozone layer, which protects against skin cancer. Another specific example is developing an electric car, which saves money on gasoline and maintenance, while at the same time not generating the exhaust pollution of internal-combustion cars. Developing hydrogen fusion or solar energy also may be examples of a less expensive and cleaner fuel for manufacturing processes.

Table 24-2 applies the generic matrix to the problem of environmental protection, especially in developing nations. The main conservative goal is economic development, and the main liberal goal is a clean environment. Conservatives also endorse a clean environment but not as much as liberals. Likewise, liberals also endorse economic development, but not as much as conservatives.

The main conservative policy is to rely on the marketplace on the theory that consumers would not buy products that are causing unhealthful pollution. The main liberal policy is to rely on anti-pollution regulation on the theory that the fines, the taxes, and other penalties will cause business to reduce pollution.

The usual result consists of compromise regulations that are not as severe as liberals would like but better than nothing. The compromise regulations are not as desirable to business as no regulation but better than what the liberals are advocating.

A win-win or SOS solution might involve public policy designed through financial and other incentives to generate new processes for manufacturing, agriculture, transportation, and energy that are more profitable to business but at the same time cleaner to the environment than previous processes. Such a profitable and clean policy would be an improvement on economic development and a clean environment.

Table 24-2. Pollution Policy

Criteria Alternatives	C Economic Development	L Clean Environment
C Marketplace	+	—
L Anti-Pollution Regulation	—	+
N Compromise Regulations	0	0
SOS Improved Manufacturing, Agricultural and Other Processes (More Profitable and Cleaner)	++	++

An example might include the use of vehicles and machines that use less gasoline and oil but are even more productive. Such innovations are easier in terms of technology, funding, and other considerations for some kinds of pollution. Such innovations may also have a bigger impact on some kinds of pollution. The optimum allocation of incentive money is a separate problem. The important consideration here is shifting conservatives and liberals toward such win-win solutions rather than toward relatively ineffective marketplace and regulatory policies.

III. Social Policy

The social policy example deals with the closely related concepts of poverty, welfare, and unemployment. A key problem in those areas is how to move difficult cases to meaningful jobs from conditions of poverty, welfare, and unemployment. A meaningful job in this context is a job that an impoverished person can be hired to perform on a long-term basis and that the impoverished person will not readily quit.

The issue here is how to find jobs for welfare recipients. The conservative emphasis is to leave it up to the recipient to find a job on his own and not make it a responsibility of other people.

The liberal emphasis is on the welfare agency or another government agency doing most of the job-finding work. The neutral position might involve delegating the activity to a non-profit organization.

A key conservative goal is to save tax money. That means encouraging job-finding to reduce the welfare payments, but not incurring high fees for job-finding. A key liberal goal is to find jobs for welfare recipients not just to save welfare payments, but also because jobs can increase the income, quality of life, and dignity of welfare recipients.

An SOS alternative is to contract out to a private profit-making firm at a commission of about $5,000 per welfare recipient who receives long-term employment. Half the commission is paid after four months on the job and the other half after eight months. The firm is responsible for providing training, day care, employment leads, advice, and dispute resolution, which the government agency might otherwise provide.

This is a good example of contracting out. The profit motive stimulates more success in finding jobs than the rate of success by a government agency or a non-profit organization. The firm also has more capability than the recipient. Tax money is saved in the long-run as a result of replacing welfare with work. It may also be saved in the short-run by costing less money per long-term job found than the cost with a government agency or non-profit organization. See Table 24-3.

Table 24-3. Finding Jobs

Goals Alternatives	C Saving tax money.	L Finding jobs.
C Up to recipients.	+	—
L Government agency.	—	+
N Non-profit organizations.	0	0
SOS or Win-Win Contracting out.	++	++

IV. POLITICAL POLICY

The political policy example relates to promoting people and other aspects of governmental personnel management. A key problem is developing criteria for promotions and merit raises, especially in the sensitive area of police procedures.

The components of the SOS package might include (1) increased police professionalism which can both reduce crime and help separate the innocent from the guilty, (2) drug medicalizatinon designed to reduce drug related crimes and abuse of those suspected of being on drugs, although drug medicalization may lack present political feasibility, and (3) rent supplements refer to providing rental subsidies to low-income applicants to facilitate economic and racial integration, which thereby tends to reduce the economic and racial discrimination that may sometimes be present in police behavior. See Table 24-4.

Table 24-4. Restraining Police

Goals / Alternatives	C Reduce crime.	L Protect innocent and guilty from abuse.
C Free hand.	+	—
L Citizens review board.	—	+
N Police review board.	0	0
SOS or Win-Win 1. Professionalism. 2. Drug medicalization. 3. 3. Rent supplement.	++	++

V. SOME CONCLUSIONS

In all four situations, providing for performance pay by public policy enables the achievement of both conservative and liberal goals:

1. Paying the stockbroker on the basis of how well the stocks do in terms of resale or dividends. That minimizes regulation and simultaneously encourages doing a good job for consumers.
2. Paying environmental research firms to develop new processes in manufacturing, transportation, energy, and agriculture that are both less expensive and cleaner than the old processes. Doing so satisfies the desire for higher profits and a cleaner environment, simultaneously.
3. Paying employment agencies commissions for finding jobs for welfare recipients and other unemployed people. The arrangement enables the public sector and taxpayers to be relieved of having to support an unemployed person who is now adding to the GNP, and the person is pleased to have the job, the income, the self-satisfaction, and other benefits.
4. Paying police bonuses beyond a minimum salary for reducing various kinds of crime within their specialty and also for making arrests that result in convictions without the police evidence being excluded. That kind of performance pay simultaneously promotes the conservative emphasis on reducing crime and the liberal emphasis on reducing violations of due process and harassment of the innocent.

Chapter 25

WIN-WIN VOUCHERS

Stuart Nagel

This chapter is organized in terms of examples from economic policy (minimum wage vouchers), technology policy (workers and farmers productivity vouchers), social policy (housing and school vouchers), and political policy (decentralized education vouchers).

I. MINIMUM WAGE VOUCHERS (TABLE 25-1)

As of 1991, business management in the Philippines argued the maximum it could afford as a minimum wage would be 90 pesos per day. Otherwise , workers would have to be laid off or not hired leading to a reduction in food, shelter, and clothing.

Labor argued that the minimum wage should be at least 100 pesos per day. Otherwise, workers would not be able to afford adequate food, shelter, and clothing.

The logical compromise would be somewhere between 90 and 100 pesos depending on the relative bargaining power of management and labor.

The SOS involves management paying 89 pesos, but the workers receive 101 pesos. The government makes up the difference of 12 pesos per day in return for management and labor activities.

To receive the 12-pesos subsidy, management must agree to hire only unemployed workers and provide them with on-the-job training to bring their skills up to the 101-pesos level. The unemployed workers must accept the job and the on-the-job training, and perform both at a passing level.

Table 25-1. The Philippine Minimum Wage Problem

Goals Alternatives	C Overpayment	L Decent wages
C 90 per day	+	-
L 100 per day	-	+
N 95 per day	0	0
SOS Or Win-Win 101 to worker, 89 from employer, 12 wage supplement	++	++

II. Pricing Food in China and Elsewhere (Table 25-2)

The intermediate totals in parentheses are based on the first three goals. The bottom line totals are based on all the goals, including the indirect effects of the alternatives.

The SOS of a price supplement involves farmers receiving 101% of the price they are asking, but urban workers and others paying only 79% which is less than the 80% that they are willing and able to pay.

The difference of 22% is made up by food stamps given to the urban workers in return for agreeing to be in programs that upgrade their skills and productivity. The food stamps are used to pay for staple products (like rice or wheat) along with cash. Farmers can then redeem the stamps for cash, provided that they also agree to be in programs that increase their productivity.

Food stamps have administrative feasibility for ease in determining that workers and farmers are doing what they are supposed to do in return for the food stamps. They cannot be easily counterfeited. They serve as a check on how much the farmers have sold.

By increasing the productivity of farmers and workers, the secondary effects occur of improving farming methods, increasing exports, increasing the importing of new technologies, and increasing the GNP.

High prices are not politically feasible because of too much opposition from workers who consume, but do not produce food. The high prices though are acceptable if they can be met by way of price supplements in the form of food stamps.

On the broader implications of the examples, food pricing illustrates the third party benefactor which can be a very useful SOS perspective for resolving conflicts between ethnic groups, economic classes, labor versus management, landlord versus tenants. Other examples include:

1. The landlord-tenant resolution with regard to rent vouchers.
2. The labor-management resolution with regard to the minimum wage.

3. The present example is rural versus urban and also seller versus consumers.
4. On the international front, the third party benefactor can be illustrated by the Camp David Accords.

Table 25-2. Simple Food Pricing

Alternatives \ Goals	C Rural well-being	L Urban well-being
C 1. High price. 60	+	-
L 1. Low price. 40	-	+
N 1. Middle price. 50	0	0
SOS or Win-Win 1. 61 to firms 2. 49 to worker (with food stamps)	++	++

III. TRAINING VOUCHERS

Table 25-3 is entitled "Central Government Versus Individuals on Training." Conservatives would like to leave the decision to individuals as to whether to get training and what training to get in order to be able to adopt to changing times, especially technologies. Liberals would like to have the government set up training programs, possibly like the Works Progress Administration of the depression years, or like the public school system, but for adults.

By leaving it to individuals to make training decisions, conservative argue that responsiveness to individual abilities and interests is more likely to be met. Leaving it to the individuals is also more likely to be responsive to market forces of supply and demand. Liberals justify a more governmental approach on the grounds that such an approach can bring everybody up to a certain level of computer literacy and knowledge of contemporary science. By raising virtually everybody above such a threshold, a desirable uniformity is obtained.

A win-win solution might involve the federal government giving a $2,000 training voucher to every man, woman, and child or at least to every adult over age 18. Such a voucher could be used to pay for whatever training each individual thought best in light of their abilities and interests and in light of the present supply and demand for people with the training the individuals pursue.

Such a policy would be highly responsive. It would also result in a high degree of training, which would not occur if people had to use their own money. Some people do not have the money available. Those who do may not be farsighted enough to spend it on training. The voucher would be worthless unless it is spent for training. It would be an earmarked voucher like a housing voucher or food stamps that could only be cashed in by accredited training programs or on-the-job training. The existence of so many vouchers would stimulate entrepreneurs to develop worthwhile training programs in order to attract the voucher holders.

Such a policy would be highly decentralized in terms of the decision-making, but yet centralized in terms of the funding. This provides the best of both in a win-win way. The winners are not only conservatives and liberals but also (1) individual trainees whose training enables them to earn higher and more satisfying incomes, (2) their trainers who make money performing a service by upgrading those individuals, (3) the government which gets more revenue from the increased gross national product more than the cost of the vouchers, (4) the children and grandchildren of the trainees who now have better role models, (5) the customers, clients, patients, and other beneficiaries of the better trained individuals, (6) the savings to the taxpayers from various forms of public aid that might be paid to the trainees who might be otherwise unemployed without the training.

Table 25-3. Central Government versus Individual Decisions on Training.

Alternatives \ Goals	C Responsiveness	L Uniformity or widespread
C Individual decisions	+	-
L Government decisions	-	+
N Both	0	0
SOS or Win-Win 1. Vouchers from gov't 2. 2. Individual decisions on how to spend the vouchers	++	++

For another example of vouchers, see the section on "Educational Integration" in Chapter 29, which discusses vouchers for elementary and secondary education.

PART SIX: BIBLIOGRAPHIES

Chapter 26

CREATIVITY BIBLIOGRAPHIES

(1) James Austin, *Chase Chance and Creativity: The Lucky Art of Novelty* (Columbia University Press, 1978).

(2) Samm Baker, *Your Key to Creative Thinking: How to Get More and Better Ideas* (Harper & Row, 1962).

(3) Stephen D. Brookfield, *Developing Critical Thinkers: Challenging Adults to Explore Alternative Ways of Thinking and Acting* (Jossey-Bass 1991).

(4) Perry W. Buffington, "Strokes of Genius," *Sky,* February 1987, p.121-125.

(5) David Campbell, *Take the Road to Creativity and Get Off Your Dead End* (Center for Creative Leadership, 1985).

(6) Coogan, William H. and Oliver H. Woshinsky, *The Science of Politics: An Introduction to Hypothesis Formation and Testing* (University Press of America, 1982).

(7) De Bono, Edward, *Lateral Thinking: Creativity Step by Step* (Harper Colophon Books, 1973).

(8) De Bono, Edward, "Thinking in America: The Lost Art," *Critical Intelligence.* October 1994, p.3-9.

(9) Dogan, Mattei and Robert Pahre, *Creative Marginality: Innovation at the Intersections of Social Sciences* (Westview Press, 1990).

(10) Harman, Willis and Howard Rheingold, *Higher Creativity: Liberating the Unconscious for Breakthrough Insights* (G.P. Putman's Sons, 1984).

(11) Harriman, Richard, *"Creativity: Moving Beyond Linear Logic,"* *The Futurist,* August 1984, p.17-20.

(12) Nierenberg, Gerard I, *The Art of Creative Thinking* (Barnes & Noble, 1996).

(13) Nuernberger, Phil, "Mastering the Creative Process" *The Futurist,* August 1984, p.33-36.

(14) Osborn, F, *Applied Imagination: Principles and Procedures of Creative Problem-Solving* (Charles Scribner's Sons, 1963).

(15) Parnes, Sidney J, "Learning Creative Behavior: Making the Future Happen" *The Futurist,* August 1984, p.30-32.

(16) Quester, George H, "Creativity and Bureaucracy: The Search for Success" *The Futurist,* August 1984, p.27-29.

(17) Rosenfeld, Robert and Jenny C. Servo, "Business and Creativity: Making Ideas Connect," *The Futurist,* August 1984, p. 21-26.

(18) Rothenberg, Albert, The Emerging Goddess: *The Creative Process in Art, Science, and Other Fields* (University of Chicago Press, 1990).

(19) Stein,Morris I. and Shirley J. Heinze, *Creativity and the Individual: Summaries of Selected Literature in Psychology and Psychiatry* (Free Press of Glencoe, 1960).

(20) Tatsuno, Sheridan M, "Japan's Move Toward Creativity" *The GAO Journal,* Summer 1990, p.13-18.

(21) Technology is Changing Basic Structure of Education" *News Report,* Summer 1993, p.2-5.

(22) Waitley, Denis E. and Robert B. Tucker, "How to Think Like an Innovator," *The Futurist,* May-June 1987, p.9-15.

(23) Weinstein, Bob, *20 Ways to be More Creative in Your Job* (Simon & Schuster, 1983).

INDEX